yeah.
no.
totally.

lisa wells

perfect day publishing
portland. oregon

a Perfect Day book
© Lisa Wells 2011
The moral right of the author has been asserted.

Yeah. No. Totally. / Lisa Wells

Printed in the U.S.A. by Brown Printing of Portland, OR.

ISBN: 978-0-9836327-0-2
Library of Congress Control Number: 2011907315

First Edition

Photo by Jaclyn Campanaro
Cover by Sumanth Prabhaker
Perfect Day logo by Corinne Manning
Website by David Small

www.perfectdaypublishing.com

for the invisible and excluded,
for future generations,
for Edie Rose.

contents

yeah. no. totally.

    an introduction   1

la luna   9

girlfriends who hate call of duty   19

tour diary   27

nicaragua diary, 2007   41

the marginal gastby   53

the same fucking day, man.   59

knell of the worried well   71

the body autumnal

    a story   83

yeah. no. totally.

an introduction

"It is said that if the future generations find out through records that we did nothing to preserve the good ways, they will pull and box our ears, and even throw us from our houses into the streets. This suffering will be of our own making. The lack of peace in our own spiritual being could trigger the revolution."

– Hopi Prophecy

Having survived an exchange of millennia, a few plastic wars, and a series of ecological holocausts, we've arrived: Portland's lattice of gentrified streets before us. We stand dumbfounded in the afternoon sun on SE 12th and Hawthorne watching this jabroni in white high-tops order from the taco cart. He is sealed in skin-tight black jeans, muffin-top bulging through ultra-romantic blue and white striped tank-top. A flaccid, jheri-curled mohawk gently sweeps his tattooed shoulders, an aggressively ironic pencil-thin moustache edges his mouth, the way a dancer's landing-strip accentuates her hole. Oh yes! The face complete with neon-green plastic sunglasses and a look of enormous self-satisfaction.

At the coffee shop next door, a girl with a pouty mouth asks the barista, "You don't drive?"

Barista says in deepest voice possible, "I've never had a license."

"Never?" asks girl, pretending to care.

"The only license I have is the license I take," he says.

Everything is parody, facsimile, reminiscent of. Earlier centuries' fashion recapitulated exponentially, decade by decade. Now they've resurrected the nineties' resurrection of the sixties; *edgy silhouettes, bright accents, and zany looks, all of which are feelin' fresh again.*

Bands are blowing up. It happens a lot these days, or at least people talk as if it does. You never know when, or to whom, it might happen. You never know when it might happen to *you*. The vague threat of success hanging in the smoke-free air of every dive bar is buying the next round of Pabst and otherwise serving as the Dutch boy's finger in the dam of social order. And everyone knows the other important story operating the system, "So-and-so got too drunk and talked shit on band-X just before they signed to Sub Pop. But *SO-and-so* played nice and now they'll tour together and play *All Tomorrow's Parties*." There are celebrities everywhere. Celebrity to a marginal world, but all the same, here they are; serving our coffee at Stumptown, drinking absinthe at Grizzly Beer, a table away.

Guys like to say – for these conversations are, by and large, had by those with the Y chromosome –

they like to say things like "I don't care what happens, I just want to play music." But everyone knows that's a lie. Everyone in Portland comes from somewhere else, and no one moves here because they *just want to play music*. Musicians with no plans to "take it public," where they exist, stick to their hometowns, to their garages and day jobs. The salt of the earth indie vibe is long over. It was dead by 2003, I'd say, when the first wave of ambitious boys in shaggy hair and prep-school blazers descended. New boy bands were forming every day, identifiable by their cool-guy slouch, their distorted vocals and down-stroke heavy git-riffs. What took hold of Portland by the fall of 2003 was careerism, plain and simple, with a grip that's almost choked us out.

Wild animal motifs are in. Actual wild animals are out.

Last night at Grizzly Beer, the minor indie-rock celebrity bar, talking to Peter. Peter in his flannel shirt and wife-beater, eyeballing the sexy young ladies. "Fucking atheist, vegan hipsters," he says. "They're all about efficiently destroying the planet. 'Eat tofu and save food for seven people?' As if we need more people! Science is the god of efficiency. God is YOUTUBE." His rants are canned, predictable. I feel as though he's speaking my thoughts aloud. All my thoughts; predictable, predestined, projected. There's no way out.

"The most amazing part," he continues, "is that none of them will admit that they're hipsters. I mean, you've got some guy in the most ironic fucking glasses talking shit on a 'hipster douche.' Incredible!"

Rumor has it that Stephen Malkmus will be playing on Grizzly Beer's bar league softball team alongside dudes from Joggers and that guy from The Shins. Someone suggests they pay extra dues on account of the psych-out advantage.

"Didn't that guy from the Shins open a taco cart?" asks Peter.

Someone fakes a snore.

Zoe approaches our table. Sweet, skinny Zoe, at one time overweight, ignored by her Kansas high school, now talking behind her fringed page-boy haircut about her opening at a Los Angeles gallery. Talks about being sick of art rock. She's into earnest music now and has recently discovered a band with a deep sound. "It's all about the lyrics," she says.

Peter smiles and nods and after she flits away admits to having almost wrecked his mom's minivan observing summertime skirts. "I need," he sighs, "I must. Get. Laid." It's the bar's subconscious speaking, a unanimous Morse code.

"Are you a hipster?" I ask.

He laughs.

When they finally gave us a name, "Generation Y," it was to return the question of their proliferation to some omniscient referee. They ask why. We say so what.

"I don't understand why we're supposed to respect our elders," the barista complains, "It's like, NO. You fucked up the entire planet and usurped all the possibility, and you want my respect? You're lucky you're allowed to walk around. I mean, the fact that I even let you live, you should be thanking me!"

Later, he texts me: "Octogenidiots."

Before the coining of Generation Y, I was hoping for "Omega." I still like the sound of it. It's more accurate. It intimates the following facts:

1. They had Cousteau. We have bleeding seas. Black with oil. Bird cadavers.

2. They got soul, they gave us disco. They gave us HPV, Parabens, hundreds of cable channels.

3. We want to drink water from the river. We want the stories they buried and the elders they weren't.

"If you remember the seventies, you weren't there." This charming bromide delivered always with cutesy smile. Amnesia once again redeems the day.

I don't remember when I first noticed. Changes that come as fast as these have a way of erasing the world before. I remember there was a time when I could go around all day, visiting all kinds of places, and not see a single person looking at a screen. Then, one day, there was an ocean of faces bathed in ghostly blue, so slack and unassuming it seemed they'd always been there. The news now washing over those faces; they found that little kid. The one who was missing. The one from the billboards. The one from the magazine. Just like we figured. His mom killed him and dumped him in the river. It's all over Facebook.

Whenever I see that little red number in the upper left-hand corner of the screen, like when there's a new message or a status update or whatever, my heart leaps and claps like a joyful child. I view my profile to see what I think of me. *Somebody. Somebody. Somebody. Please.*

la luna

In the spring of 1990 I was eight, and my father and mother had recently separated. The rain didn't let up for months. The days were so dark that looking at the sky one had difficulty telling the time, or if the sun had even risen. Typical weather for Portland. At the time, my dad was a drummer in a butt-rock band. He'd been drumming since he was a child, a Ringo enthusiast, but prior to the butt-rock fad had failed to locate *his movement*. I'd grown up observing band practice in our basement. I'd lie on the rug with my crayons and listen, thoughtfully giving each song a score in my giant kid's tablet, pretending I was a *Star Search* judge. During the day, sometimes I'd sneak down and decipher song lyrics scrawled in black sharpie on yellow legal pad: songs about women who make men moan, urges and needs, exhaustive metaphors relating the narrator's body to that of a sports car. That spring his band Thunderhead was going to play The

Pine Street Theater, an all-ages venue, and I'd finally have the chance to see him perform in public.

I trailed him around the house while he got ready for the gig, stood behind him in the mirror as he flipped his permed mane back and forth against the hairdryer's stream in a campaign to produce maximum body. He wore leather capris, the perforated seams lined with fringed leather, and a cropped Special Forces tank top that featured a skull in a green beret and the slogan "Mess with the best, die like the rest." In my new black bowler hat, descending the stairs at his side, I felt pretty cool, though I'm certain that to the gum-smacking door girl, the sight of a middle-aged rocker dragging his eight-year old daughter into the viscous depths was a rather pathetic display of a dream on dialysis.

I asked Dad to make sure they played "Kiss Me Where It Hurts," one of the few songs they took into the studio. The final mix included a woman's scolding voice and cracking whips. Before that song I didn't know women could hurt men. It was always the other way around. The women who raised me seethed, they didn't make demands, and they certainly didn't perpetrate violence. The prospect interested me. In the canted blue and pink stage lights curdling with smoke, Barry the frontman sashayed with the flagging, drunken flair of a bored stripper.

The sampler issued a profusion of whip cracks and as his voice strained toward the highest octaves he gripped the mic with one hand and his balls with the other. Not for emphasis, the way his idols did, but continuously, perhaps in lieu of an instrument. In the calamitous basement of memory — that voice, those soft blond locks and distended belly — he remains; a contemporary castrati.

Rearranging my hat in the bathroom mirror, I overheard a pair of stiletto-heeled boots call out to the neighboring stall, "Yeah, but the drummer's hot. I'd fuck the drummer," and felt a twinge of pride. (Had I any loyalty to my mother? One wonders.) Minutes later, when she appeared in the mirror, leather-jacket clad, fingering the lipstick from her teeth, she said, "Great hat!" and I thought I'd die from love.

The owners of Seattle's RCKCNDY took over Pine Street in 1992 and named it La Luna. It's this incarnation of the club I remember best. Four years after my first visit, I returned un-chaperoned for my thirteenth birthday party. I didn't care who was playing. The point was to be at a show. We were a large group of girls emerging giddily from two minivans, and were immediately taunted by older teens waiting in the ticket line. "Thanks for the ride, mommy," they snickered.

Inside the club, the vaguely-titled post-grunge genre "alternative" shook from the stacks flanking the stage. We negotiated the venue the way we did any other, by forming a closed seated circle, crisscross applesauce, on the dingy floor. In meticulously torn fishnet stockings and ten-eyed Doc Martin knock-offs, passing a stolen Marlboro Light 100, piercingly self-conscious. That night, Grrl rock legends Sleater-Kinney played, still just girls themselves. We stared in awe as they screamed and beat the hell out of their instruments and tried to remain standing while all around us men slammed into each other. At one point, frontwoman Corin Tucker stopped mid-scream and said to the crowd, "Fuck your mosh-pit. This isn't a fucking frat party, assholes." Then invited *all the ladies* to join her for some dancing on stage. I realized I didn't know how to dance at the exact moment my cronies boosted me up. "It's her birthday!" they yelled and I smiled and nervously pushed my hair behind my ears, then pogoed in place for the duration.

One weeknight in the fall of my freshman year of high school, I wandered down for a balcony show, a much smaller room above the main venue, reserved for world or folk acts. The schticky English crooner Ben Lee was headlining. He wrote songs about sitcoms and cereal. I'd heard he was cute and just a little older than me, so I paid the five bucks and joined some kids I recognized from school at a candlelit table near the stage. The girl next to me, a junior, was determined to bed Ben Lee, and spent an hour outside the stage door after the show, chain-smoking cloves, trying to cajole him into "having soup" with her. Was this the beginning of the awkward indie-girl fad?

I felt sorry for the opening act, a saddish guy with acne scars and greasy hair hunched over an acoustic guitar. It seemed to me he might be homeless. We were four of twenty audience members, most of whom had wandered in drunk and were simply waiting for him to finish. The singer almost whispered, but as I strained to hear above the chatter a scope opened and focused between us. The song was familiar, a muffled engine of sorrow that inflicted me with grief and somehow also with pleasure. The final words of a bedridden pneumoniac who can't lift his head from the pillow but can, in his limited way, hope against hope. *My internal life exactly!*

Turns out I wasn't alone in that sentiment. One year later I came with hundreds of others to see the same guy perform, this time at the main venue downstairs. In the interim, the movie *Good Will Hunting* had been released and one of his songs on the soundtrack was up for an Oscar. He lost out to Celine Dion's "My Heart Will Go On" but his trajectory was fixed and I tasted bitter ash, leaping with all my strength to catch glimpses of him above the heads of those *poseurs*. I wanted to slug them and scream, "Where were you last year?" Horseshit, of course, considering I hadn't even heard his name before that night the year before. My good fortune in that accidental audience dawned on me after twenty leaping minutes, when the confusing spectacle of an opiate-addled Elliott Smith swerved from the stage without having completed a single song.

Eventually I was one of the older girls grilling the tweeners in line at the club. Chain-smoking Camel Lights purchased with a friend's ID. Nearly every Friday and Saturday night we'd speed from the suburbs toward punk shows in my H.S. boyfriend's CRX. He was a devoted young man whose dubious claims of Irish ancestry found him perpetually drunk and pumping his fist to Pogue Mahone. His slurred lectures turned me on to zines, LSD, and Lookout! Records, among other things. As a duo, we were quite popular and were frequently ejected from the club for attempting to enter by tripping down the stairs or because we'd projectile vomited alcohol all over the bathroom. The rules of belonging had become clear to me; skip the opener, share your hooch covertly, give cigarettes to kids if they ask, don't talk too loud during ballads, support the band you came to see (dance if you can, otherwise tap your foot and nod your head in approval,) buy the 7-inch. An oblique morality drove everything we did. Devotion to music, to our friends, to secondhand clothes. A kind of 1950's take on romance and fidelity to your one true love. Jokes perpetual. Walkman over Discman. Vinyl above all. Hoodies over leather. High top chucks. Obscure foreign films. Forties of Beast Ice. The limits so precise as to annihilate all existential anxiety. Even then I knew it, could sense that one day I'd end up here, a boring old lady paralyzed with ambivalence.

After H.S., I moved to Seattle for a while and was living there when La Luna finally closed. Its absence continues to nag me, as if I haven't registered it on a somatic level. Now, more than a decade later, I pass Ninth and Pine overcome with the sudden paranoia that this is not quite my city.

The ceremony of going to shows is part of what I think about when I think about growing up in Portland. Shows and house parties and this exhausting fixation on having fun all the time. It's an ideal still hotly pursued by some friends who are well into their thirties. In Portland, such a pursuit is encouraged.

A city whose mayor recently commissioned a rather hyperbolic portrait of Modest Mouse frontman Isaac Brock to hang in his office in city hall. And Pink Martini frontman Thomas Lauderdale enjoys some influence in local politics and occasionally performs with the Oregon Symphony. And local filmmakers only ever cast minor indie-rock celebrities, and generally, the city's obsession with its eccentric rock-and-roll identity has doubled-back on satire.

Bitter ash. Oh, well. Whatever it is, there's always the next thing.

girlfriends who hate call of duty

this is a group for all the girlfriends who hate Call of Duty, who end up boyfriend-less due to their boyfriends becoming addicted to online massacres

I don't have a boyfriend who plays video games but I joined this Facebook group hoping to learn what was so appealing about the game *Call of Duty*.

> "i lost my boyfriend to call of duty ... and im afraid my next bf might do it to me again help me, avoid this!"

> "sorry for all the losses. and finding a guy without a game system is probably a tricky thing. once one of my bf's friends got one, they ALL got one. its a vicious chain."

> "does anyone elses b/f all of a sudden start trying to speak gangsta when they play. im in VA we all have a country accent, but i swear he thinks he's an online god, and begins to talk with the worst fake Brooklyn accent ive ever heard"

I learned about the group from a friend who had, over the year, lost her boyfriend to *COD 2: Modern*

Warfare. Her boyfriend the green-builder. The pacifist hippie. What started as a lark between a few friends had spun quickly out of control. Now they texted each other inside jokes constructed by game play at all hours of the night. Everyone bought headsets, and a big screen TV was moved in. In the beginning, he only played at night after smoking a blunt. Now it's all the time. He even wakes up early on weekends to play after making coffee. "I come downstairs, and it's fucking World War III in my living room," my friend tells me.

I want to interview her guy about the appeal of the game, but she claims he's too humiliated to talk. I had her ask him for a few examples of player names. He admits there are a lot of homophobic handles, which makes him uncomfortable. Apparently there are also a couple of gentlemen in the world who've selected the respective monikers "Ilynchblackpeople" and "Jewkiller." If one wishes to play Army Man realistically, this might be a start.

One wonders about the outcomes of such repetitive stimulus. I had a friend who played the game *Hitman* every day over a period of some months. As you might have guessed, the objective of the game is to kill assigned targets. For a while, in real life, whenever people tilted their heads in this particular way, like one of the targets in the game, my friend was hijacked by the impulse to blow their brains out.

Recently, on the other side of the existential echo-chamber, a group of soldiers made news for having been denied Purple Hearts even though they'd incurred traumatic brain injuries when a rocket exploded outside their housing trailer in Bagdad. The trippy thing is, it happened while they were playing *Call of Duty*. If you're a soldier, please forgive my surprise. I realize life in a war zone is not constant combat, that there's a lot of downtime and slim pickings on distraction. But to a civilian mind like mine, this seems akin to, I don't know, watching NatGeo in the woods, or shushing your lover when he puts the moves on because you're busy "reading" porn.

I would now like to submit a quote for your consideration, the speaker of which we'll soon get to know more intimately. "It's almost like a religious experience to see a battlefield. To hear the explosions — to see a person bleeding out and die — see everything on fire and smell the smoke and burning flesh. It makes you truly realize what it is to be alive. Combat is the biggest rush you can have." [1] — Kentucky Kenny

1 Dave Phillips, The Colorado Springs Gazette, *Casualties of War, Part I: The hell of war comes home*, July 25, 2009.

Eastridge, a mean-eyed and flap-eared private from the 12th infantry. Kenny might be describing the snap from a disassociated logical mind into pure being, or the rush one gets from approximated danger via a television screen. In any case, it's evident he derives some pleasure from it. *Call of Duty* doesn't duplicate a combat zone, it would be ridiculous to suggest it does (except to potential customers). The stakes are lower, obviously, and it fails to generate the same adrenalized state as a near-death situation. Then again, with so many soldiers surviving, returning again and again to the battlefield doped and in the throes of dissociative trauma, maybe even actual near-death situations fail at feeling real.

Another boy in Kenny's battalion says he joined up because the Army's commercials made it seem like a cool job, all the guns and black helicopters. Kenny chose the infantry because "That's where you get to do all the awesome stuff." Like what kind of awesome stuff, Kenny? Like shooting up a family barbeque full of Iraqi civilians sound-tracked by some heavy-metal "killin' music." In the version he tells, families were picnicking and playing soccer. A couple of old men were chatting under the shade of a tree. He fired toward the crowd, which caused everyone to panic and flee in their cars. But there was a driving ban in effect, an excuse to open up on anyone who started their engine, and that's what he did.

Back home in Colorado Springs, a string of murders is traced back to soldiers at Fort Collins, including Kenny and others from his battalion. Two fellow soldiers are executed, one in a parking lot, on his knees begging for his life, another on his birthday after a heavy dose of apple schnapps. A young civilian couple is shot to death while setting up signs for a yard sale. An older man is shot while walking to get gas for his truck. A random 19-year-old nursing student is run over, then stabbed repeatedly with a combat knife. According to Kenny, "The Army pounds it into your head until it is instinct: kill everybody, kill everybody. And you do. Then they just think you can just come home and turn it off."

How is our military handling this disturbing trend of random violence? There's psychological counseling available for soldiers suffering from PTSD and other disorders (you may have to wait a month for an appointment and will forever after be known to your comrades as *Shitbag*.) They're also trying out a flagship intervention named, dystopically enough, "Warrior Optimization Systems" or WAROPS, a "resiliency training" program in which soldiers learn to alleviate combat stress with deep breathing exercises and positive visualization. Presumably this method compliments bayonet training in which would-be soldiers stab dummies while the sergeant screams, "What makes the grass grow?" And everyone screams back, "Blood! Blood! Blood!"

They say you're more likely to be struck by lightning than brutally murdered by a random stranger, but it seems to me a pointless comparison. Lightning is eerily beautiful, and to my mind, one of the more magnificent natural forces on earth. To die by lightning would be like winning the lottery. Lightning, as opposed to, say, being sport-hunted by rogue U.S. soldiers returned from Fallujah, is in my book a preferable mode of expiration.

It's an expectation of surviving the era that we acquire a sophisticated callousness about matters like these. If one can't respond to horror by tossing off some sardonic quip, doubtful you'll be invited to another dinner party. *So and so is SO paranoid. Avoiding blind alleys and military personnel. It's like, life's too short, ya know?* Maybe. If you're unlucky. It's the *unrealness* of it all that troubles me, the slapstick murder playing on every screen. My yoga teacher says that concerning oneself with such human-rendered nightmares invites them into your life. But I doubt those Iraqi kids were ruminating being gunned down while playing soccer, or that Colorado Springs teenager, on her way to school. And doubtful that positive thinking would have innoculated them from what happened.

Think positively! What you think about, you bring about! That might be a Bradley thundering in the distance. Then again, it might just be thunder.

tour diary

wrapped in a dirty banana
blanket with

panther

The van contains the following: one snare with a busted head, two matching white leather bags, four men's magazines, three iPods, two backpacks, a large gold and red bedspread, a suitcase of CDs and T-shirts, an envelope of cash, a one-hitter meant to resemble a cigarette, a half-drained fifth of Jim Beam, a box of Emergen-C "Heart Health" (black cherry, belonging to Joe, presumably to fend off a second heart-attack), two shave kits, and the tour book.

The air-conditioning makes the van overheat but the windows roll down and actually the whole box doesn't smell too bad.

I ask Charlie if I have permission to write about him.

"Sure," he says, thoughtfully. "I read *The Paris Review* once."

"Oh yeah?" I say.

"Yeah. Some guy wrote a poem about the beauty of a lacrosse game ... what an asshole."

PORTLAND, WONDER BALLROOM

Charlie warms up on his devices, jumping up and down like a boxer before the bell. He makes robot arms while his feet crisscross under him, white tennis shoes gleaming. He mimes that his voice is a bird released from his mouth. He paces, picks up objects, takes hold of his own sweater from the stack, studies it, then throws it over his shoulder in an *everything must go!* gesture. Sometimes the mic switches hands so fluidly it looks like it's floating.

Charlie moves from the stage into the audience. A guy in the front row tries to look bored. Portland, one-time Mecca, rife with amateurs and sycophants. They came from the yawning mediocrity of Middle America, steeped in the canon of rock and roll. Not in pursuit of tedious debate on 1970's guitarists at the wine bar, but because they were in love with something. Because the music kept them awake at night, electric with desire. It's becoming clear that the honeymoon is over. Everyone's arms are folded over the fact of it, like spoiled teens at a mall Santa's knee. The cliché of total-body demolition, in green rooms and on the couches of strangers, so oft-realized we barely notice we're staring down the wounded mouth of death. The strange and specific communion with oblivion through song, now so common and executed so often that we do not meet it with more than a dulled sense of entitlement.

I captain the gold Chevy the night I join the tour. Charlie's gone home. Joe, mush-mouthed, half in the bag, wants to go to strippers. I detect his high from behind my post at the merch table, when, in receiving some information meant for the ear, I meet his boozy breath an inch from my mouth. "I'm gunna take somea tha guysfrom architcshur to stripperss. Come on Lisaaaaa ... yur tha tur managsher now."

Joe wants to PARTAY. Even after the room empties and the fluorescents dawn crudely overhead, he traverses the ballroom floor leaning, glass in hand, slurring loudly from his canted Wisconsin grin. I'm led under his arm to various special access rooms where we pause for a moment in each doorway, Joe mumbling at some employed man, mid-task, frozen in confusion.

SAN DIEGO, HOUSE OF BLUES

Charlie leans toward the audience, toward all fifteen faces, and in a lispy baritone whispers, "You're all little angels, you're my special little angels."

Q. Why do you like Panther?

A. Cuz they're really cute.

Q. You think they're pretty cute huh?

A. Mmm, Yeah.

Q. Do you want to get with them?

A. Yeah ... we'd like that.

Q. Did you like their music?

A. Yeah ... we LOVE The Panthers.

Q. Cool.

A. Heeheeheheheeheheheheheheheehe.

Q. How old are you?

A. At least eighteen.

SAN FRANCISCO TO SAN DIEGO

We don't listen to music in the van. We don't talk about music. Occasionally Charlie interrupts the silence to discuss Panther's future sound. "Let's Dance!" he says, referring to the Bowie song. Now he thinks he might find a female Rhodes player, cut his Fleetwood Mac record.

Having purgatoried their bodies with absolute focus for two decades in the name of it, they've not just tired of conversation about music, they resent music itself. Maybe they power-up an iPod for a song or two, off genre. "Words of Love" by The Mamas and the Papas elicits such high praise as, "This is good."

Charlie's burnout detector is in full effect. Joe has been grinding his teeth and glaring into the blacktop for about three days straight. I watch the window and shift my weight back and forth between my numb butt cheeks. Time for Charlie to avert the apocalypse of his project.

"Thanks for driving!" he yells at Joe, over the fanbelt.

"What?"

"Vegetarian burritos for everyone!" he screams.

PHONE CALL TO ARCHITECTURE IN HELSINKI,
2:15 AM

Gus: Hullo?

Joe: You wanna get weird?

Gus: What's that, mate?

Joe: Let's get real weird.

Gus: ...

Joe: You wanna FUCK AROUND?????

Gus: Who's this again?

Joe: I wanna fuck around!

Gus: Joe?

Joe: Let's fuck arooouuunnnddd!!!!

SAN FRANCISCO, THE FILLMORE

Charlie zips around like a hummingbird, flipping the hair from his face. A circle of girls has gathered, drawn round his charisma like tramps to a fire. He gesticulates wildly, makes sweeping generalizations, speaks impassioned nonsense. He seems to draw energy from all sources simultaneously, from the air, from the girls. Every cell of his body vibrates. He's a struck tuning fork. And because he draws on all that surrounds him, one is instantly pulled into his gravity, to orbit as an auxiliary reflection of his brilliance.

"Whaddaya think?" he asks, lighting the one-hitter. "Whitesnake's 'Here I Go Again' performed as a duet, on soprano sax and piccolo flute."

Lots of riffing.

Whiskey is "Panther spinach," ala Popeye. Charlie gets high then slugs back the dregs of the Beam bottle. When his anxiety is unlaced he slips into his full charm. More people gather around. He likes their attention now but soon enough he'll sober up. Then the paranoia. Everyone judging him. Picking him over.

We wake buzzing with adrenaline on six hours of drunken sleep and shower and climb in the van. The highway proffers a thousand paper burgers.

Joe sums it up on his blog:

> Hey you want to know what touring the United States in a rock band is like? First, pack as much random shit into a vehicle as you can in no order, including dirty blankets, rotten bananas, empty beverages, sesame seeds, dust and cell phones. Then, all you have to do is drive. All. Day. Every. Day.
>
> Better yet, just wrap yourself in a dirty banana blanket with your cell phone and the loudest fan you can find and sit in an uncomfortable chair for 10 hours a day for 6 weeks. That is 90% of the deal. VERY GLAMOROUS!

We load in, wait to sound check. Sometimes, mercifully, the rider includes a vegetable tray. Usually stale tortilla chips. Joe and Charlie start drinking, because they feel like shit and need to play. And at

8:00pm, despite all physical and mental deterioration, they manage to execute an energetic set for a crowd of ten teenagers. I sell two t-shirts. They load out. Whoever we were meant to stay with that night is drunk and would like to 'parttttyyyyyyy!!!' We look at each other gravely, climb in the van and drive again.

Between gas and the Motel 6 they'll blow most of their guarantee. Chase Benadryl with whiskey and fall asleep against the warm glow of Adult Swim. Tomorrow will bring a mind-numbing replication of this day, and every day after, until the tour ends or somebody dies.

"And the worst part is," Joe tells me, "I'll get home and be depressed."

SANTA CRUZ, THE RIO

Hangover, DT's, depression, self-loathing: all overcome in an instant! The group mind uprights in a sudden display of youthful joy. A drink does it, or the arrival of a potential fuck, or the atmospheric dope of unanimity. A one-minded and contagious lust for self-destruction swells in the club and everyone becomes their biggest, most terrible self.

Charlie sleepwalks. One minute he's crippling around like a bag of bricks and the next he's the most fun guy you've ever met. In the morning he'll be a piece of shit again, and that evening wake from his exhaustion in the sweet dawn of whiskey.

Joe is more intentional. A resolve colonizes his body and moves on the bottle, the swallowing perfunctory, and then ... presto! Wasted party guy arrives. This happens in Santa Cruz. I look up from the merch table and see them all pacing around with mischievous little grins, bottles in hand: Joe, Charlie, and some of the guys from Architecture. The tour manager, Pete, summons me to the door of the theatre. Glass Candy is on stage.

"Watch," he says, and a gigantic, blinding spotlight turns on Johnny Jewel. "Joe's playing with the spotlight," he smiles, pointing to the back stage entrance where two fat-necked club guys haul ass up the stairs as if pursued by fire.

The merch crew is throwing a wall ball down the hallway when another bouncer comes running.

"NO BALLS," he erupts, breathless.

Everyone blinks at him. He squats and wheezes.

"Okay," someone giggles, "no balls."

"No balls," we repeat in chorus.

ARGUMENT IN THE VAN: A PLAY IN ONE ACT.

JOE occupies the driver's seat. He's clearly intoxicated. CHARLIE, stoned, climbs in the back of the van.

LISA: Maybe I should drive.

JOE: I'mm finne.

CHARLIE: Seriously Joe, I don't think you should drive.

LISA: You're pretty drunk.

JOE: I'm fine. Where are we going?

CHARLIE: I think Pete hates us.

JOE: Pete doesn't hate us.

CHARLIE: Pete doesn't hate YOU. You're the spotlight guy.

CHARLIE lights the one-hitter and shoves the busted snare under the blanket.

JOE: Oh thas good, dude.

CHARLIE: What?

JOE: Thas how you broke it in the firs place.

CHARLIE: Whatever, dude. If you wanna be mad at me, be mad at me.

JOE: Dude! What are you talking about? Yurr the one who wis such a fucking dick to me this morning.

CHARLIE: Dude, what the fuck?

JOE: In tha mexsickan restaurant. I had to take a shit, dude, and you're all, 'you're so fucking slow."

After a long silence, CHARLIE sighs.

CHARLIE: Poor Garfunkle.

MOTEL 6

Joe was 25 when he had his heart attack. I heard about it before I knew him. A beautiful young idiot told me one night at a bar. In her version, the event was romantically linked to excessive cocaine use. Dreamily she told me that this guy, the one who had the heart attack (sigh) was in an *ahmazing* band that was going to "blow the fuck up." Turns out the heart attack came by way of a rare infection. Because he was just 25 years old and miraculously capable of driving himself to the ER, the staff assumed he was a tweaker, and left him alone in a dark room to calm down. After much swearing and pleading on his part, a nurse finally stopped by and administered a blood test. Next thing he knew the lights were on and a flock of white smocks descended. They snaked a tiny camera up through his pelvis into his chest. Hours later he woke in an anesthetized stupor to the image of his heart slapping around its cage. He's since given up smoking and drinks green tea instead of coffee. Plus about a bottle of Monopolowa every night, because *hey, you gotta live a little.*

Presently, he's passed out on the bed next to me, his mouth slack, his moustache moist and glistening. Charlie's on the other bed, fetal, his dark hair matted with sweat, his face somehow alert in sleep, like something weak and beaten listening for the door. The world spoils its gifted with compliments, smiles on their tyrannies, placates their frustrations, then turns to loathe them in secret. I don't envy him.

Under this motel, concrete; and under that scab, the land. A single pulse. From the cum-stained black box of the Troubadour to the imperial balconies of the Fillmore, we can't help but be of one mind. Just as the women cleaning the room where we've chased Benadryl with whiskey are singing; so are we, from our atolls of isolation, singing. The song of whatever it is to be living, in a particular skin, one among many, animated by the great pulse of the land. A record of our attempts. All the awful driving toward immortality.

nicaragua diary, 2007

December 21st. The narrow streets are packed shoulder to shoulder with shoppers, plastic Christmas trees twinkle, and a white man called Santa stands on the corner waving. It's 105 degrees outside. The little shops blast reggaeton and hock red plastic sleds though hardly anyone in this country will ever lay eyes on snow. I'm sweating, furiously pushing through the crowd, wishing I'd never come here. It was the pot farmer who convinced me. In the dishroom of the bar where I scoured pitchers. Every year I planned to stay in Portland and really build a life, buy bookshelves, develop an exercise routine, host craft nights, etc. But every year the winter arrived and I'd spend too much time in bars, sleep with the wrong men, hate my job, have a meltdown and leave again. As anyone who's backpacked through tropical countries knows, there can be such a thing as *too much* paradise, and after just a few months, I'd lay on a white beach dreaming of the bike I'd buy back in Portland, all the literary events I'd attend, Swiss Chard, the color I'd paint my walls. One miserably heavy Schwinn and zero cultural events later, and I was planning a trip to Mexico. Good exchange rate, promiscuous Europeans. Such was my cycle.

"You gotta go to Nicaragua, man, it's cheaper, and everyone there's a poet," the pot farmer told me. That sounded pretty good to me. It was all the thinking I did on it, meaning I didn't think at all.

I've been renting a room in León since October, above a homeless outreach office. One of the street kids, Juan María, sleeps in the computer room below me, and through the giant gaps in the hardwood floor I watch him pray. My Spanish is shitty, and I'm constantly offended by phrases he tosses at me on my way to the bathroom we share. One time I think he's hitting me up for booze when really he's asking, when did you get home? I shrug and hand him the dregs of my Gato Negro bottle.

"Oye, Juan María," I sometimes say, "why don't you scrub up your piss puddle?" But the puddle isn't his alone. By seven a.m., after fireworks, bus horns, a thousand screaming roosters, and the morning alarm (a five-minute city-wide wake-up call resembling a sort of air raid siren) the street level of the house crowds with kids who've come to build props for their winter play. This year, they'll be covering the history of Spanish colonization and the subjugation of indigenous populations in roughly 45 minutes. The play's director, Don Mañuel, has tasked them with the construction of thirty cardboard swords, forty-five loincloths, a thirty-foot dragon, and a ten-foot sparkling crucifix, but in true Charlie Brown pageant fashion, when I look in on their progress they're dancing in the kitchen. Everything's backwards in Nicaragua. It's 105 degrees Christmas week, and instead of Vince Guaraldi and the Peanuts dance, they bump and grind to reggaeton.

The leader of the pack is a kid named Angel, a salsa instructor hailing from one of the world's worst barrios. In the last few months he's developed muscles, a sparse crop of facial hair, and the deep rasp of a newly dropped voice. I don't like him. Not only because he sports a molester stash and distracts the kids from their task, but because of the way he touches Talia the blond volunteer from Belgium. *And* he asked me "Qué onda?" in front of all the kids before I knew what it meant. I just stared at him like an idiot while they all laughed and laughed.

I finally visit his barrio the day before New Year's break. I have plans to leave that evening for the touristy beach town of San Juan Del Sur, and

I'm wearing a new summer frock over my bikini. A deeply inappropriate wardrobe choice for Adiact as it turns out.

It's a place of force, a crosshatch of deeply-rutted dirt roads dotted by makeshift shelters and starving dogs. The shacks consist of four poles stapled with black plastic and sheet metal foraged from the dump. We turn down a dirt path and there's Angel, sitting on a soda crate outside the single-room shanty he shares with his mom and brothers, absorbing the full heat of the day. He's clearly embarrassed when he sees that I've accompanied the director, and I flush and stare at the ground in sympathy. He'll be our escort and security until dusk and then we have to leave. Gringos are forbidden to enter the barrio beyond the ambit, even during daylight hours. There are parts of the interior Angel hasn't even seen for fear of breaching gang boundaries.

We're guided into one of these hot black plastic shacks. It's dark and doesn't smell too good. Lengths of extension cord, rigged to the communal electric, keep a fan oscillating on the dirt floor. My eyes adjust on a bed where a blurry woman turns out of her covers with a weak moan. Her mother, Norita, brings me closer. Gently, she pushes back her daughter's matted hair and smoothes it down. Tumors are visible under the woman's skin, even in that dim light. Norita takes my hand in hers and we pray. I don't believe in God, especially not today, but I'm not telling her. Outside the shack in the blazing day, the director hands her some money to pay for a morphine drip and cab fare to the clinic.

For this reason and others, I find it difficult to enjoy the white sands and crashing surf of San Juan Del Sur. The gringos are out in force and drunk as skunks, and the locals are losing their patience. Relations between Nicas and ex-pats are strained by the recent conviction of a gringo charged with brutally murdering his local girlfriend. She was the town darling and a beauty queen until they discovered her bound in the back of the dress shop where she worked, raped and stabbed, her mouth gagged and stretched in a perpetual scream. The brutality of the murder was like nothing they'd ever seen before, except, perhaps, on American TV and it took their breath away. Grieving mobs have been forming. Alleys of eyes train on and track all gringos. This, in combination with the holiday inebriety, makes walking around any time of day feel downright dangerous.

I spend New Year's Eve on the beach thinking about Angel and Adiact. Trying to tell the Belgian volunteers that I'm going to hunt down the CEOs of the companies who polluted this country and force them to drink their own insecticide. This grouching is tolerated briefly before I am dragged back to the hostel for ceviche and for my own dose of chemical.

At 11:45, I'm dancing with a law student from Managua. Earlier, in another bar, I watched from a different table as he took off his wedding ring. We're body to body in the gated sand below the stage, trying not to look at each other. The reggaeton is so loud it strikes me dumb and my seven short-poured Cuba Libres are finally coming on.

Reggaeton is snare-heavy digital dancehall combined with Spanish rap and melodic hooks that sound as if they're being sung through a Compaq Presario. The dance most commonly performed to reggaeton is known as Perreo ("doggy-style") and can only be described as dry humping or "sexo con ropa." Typically, a woman in extremely short shorts, the kind we called "coochie cutters" in 7th grade, bends over and shakes her butt cheeks at her dance partner. The shaking is rapid but precise: a skill mastered in the western world by urban strippers and a select group of NYU dance majors. The vibration is an invitation for the man to mount her from behind, waving his plastic cup in the air and nodding his head rhythmically in approval. I don't attempt the move, though thanks to yoga, I am now capable of touching my toes. The lawyer doesn't seem to mind and offers his leg for me to mount. In my periphery, a man pushes a drunken gringa against a porta-potty wall, presses his mouth into hers and shoves his hand in her dress. The sea of dancers swells, a hoop of Dionysian graphic rolling past my eyes.

The crowd starts counting down and the lawyer makes his move, his mouth as sloppy as my grandmother's after her stroke. I push him away and wipe the spittle from my cheek. *Siete ... seis.* He laughs and stumbles at me again. *Vamos, nena. Sé amable.* But I dodge out of the way and pretend to watch for fireworks. *Cuatro ... tres.* the lawyer grabs me by my shoulders and calls me a puta. I've slipped out of my shoes and want to retrieve them from the sand before I lose them, but his wrists are boxing me in. I can't move my head to look.

I'd like to feel this kind of entitlement, I think, even just once, toward my own body. The crowd roars and I spit his saliva onto his cheek. It's a complicated feeling, absorbing such tremendous energy. Hot rage blooming in his face, and in the sky behind him a million exploding stars.

We think it's a hangover for the first twelve hours, but by the sixteenth I can no longer drag myself to the toilet by my own strength, and we begin to suspect ceviche poisoning. There's a terrible image of a shrimp haunting my mind's eye each time I wretch. My skin is freezing cold in spite of the heat and my face is drained of color save for two pink rings under my eyes. The Belgians call a cab to take me from the hostel to the local clinic. The cabby actually has to come inside and ferry me out in his arms like a bride. At the clinic, they lay me on a cot with an ill-fitting sheet. Where it pulls back from the mattress I see stains and am sick again. The doctor gives me an anti-emetic and drains two bags of saline into my vein while I sleep. Baby cries from beyond the partition keep pulling me back. I want to go home. The word hurts. Self-pity sobs out in restrained little convulsions, *home, home, home.*

It's a relief to enter the office a few days later, back in León. To wade through the cardboard swords, over the dragon, under the crucifix, to ascend the stair, cluttered with loincloths, and set down my bag in my little room above the dancing children. Portland would be a bigger relief, but in the meantime I've made this place mine. It's the same process every time. You go out into the world, get knocked around, and whatever hole you retreat to becomes *home.*

Angel stays late after rehearsal to give me salsa lessons and help me with my Spanish. I'm no natural dancer but still he regards my moves with generous enthusiasm, as if I were really blowing his mind. I manage not to trip him on the turn, for example, and he snaps his fingers and yells "Chido, chido!" In exchange for his kindness he gets to be seen in public with a gringa, less a credit to me than to colonialism. In this country so thoroughly fucked by American foreign policy, consorting with the enemy is admired.

Also, we've become friends.

When the night of the big performance arrives, I take his hand and smile and tell him "tranquilo" to help soothe his stage fright. We're on a bench in the Parque Central in front of the largest Catholic cathedral in Central America. I smear red paint from a plastic tub on his face, three stripes across each cheek, like a cat's lash, and tell him he looks strong. Don Mañuel gives the signal and the children line up. Crowds are gathering at the edge of the roped square. Families have arrived from the outlying barrios, grandparents and aunts and cousins, some having walked more than 15 miles in annihilating heat to watch the play. Dusk comes on and a drum begins.

The children emerge dressed as indigenous warriors, in loincloths and body paint and spend the first twenty minutes or so performing various perplexing rites to appease the sun and moon and "naturaleza." Eventually, Christopher Columbus enters, played by one of the blonder children, dressed in silky bloomers and white gym socks hiked up to his knees. The crowd hushes. "We have arrived with the cross," says Columbus, as three small boys heft the sparkling crucifix, already losing its structural integrity. The boys adopt yogic poses to keep the top-heavy cross from bending in half, and succeed for the most part.

Some of the taller children hold a white bed-sheet in front of a lamp and the silhouettes of three sinister ships sail into view. The Niña, Pinta, and Santa María are announced in turn, like debutantes. The conquerors arrive on the tribe, slaying the men and enslaving the women. Pandemonium ensues, the cross falls apart, and suddenly the sky is struck with bells. The players and audience freeze, confused, as it's just 36 minutes after the hour. We all crane our necks toward the tower high above, where two small boys yank the rope with all their might in tandem. Altar boys. The bells bong and bong for a full five minutes. Everyone forgets the play, their plans, their names. More people gather in the square, disoriented, and look to the faces aimed at the tower for answers, but find none. I spy Don Mañuel on the church steps, his face calm and mouth torqued, fighting a smile. I cross the square and go to him. "It's the Bishop," he yells, "protesting our 'anti-Catholic message.'" He gestures to our audience, now doubled thanks to the bells, and smiles. When they finally stop ringing, as abruptly as they began, the children resume their scene, running each other through with cardboard swords, screaming for the Catholic God or for the earth. Don Mañuel folds his arms over his chest like a warlord, proudly surveying the square. And in some hidden tower, no doubt, the Bishop congratulates himself.

Then Angel, the great warrior, emerges, his muscled torso painted with images of the sun and moon, and the crowd cheers. He draws his sword high above his head. "You will suffer for what you've done," he tells the white men, and we all hope it's true.

the marginal gatsby

" 'Whenever you feel like criticizing anyone,' he told me, 'just remember that all the people in this world haven't had the advantages you have.'" Page one. *The Great Gatsby*. This passage very carefully underlined in wavering pen, how a line strays in proportion to our concentration on keeping it straight. Someone other than Nick Carraway meditated long on this advice.

I prefer used books for this reason. A new book with clean margins means entering a conversation with the de facto expert, the author, and how boring is that? Of course the author knows the counsel delivered by Nick's father has profoundly influenced Nick's character. He rigged it that way. But this anonymous author of the margins and I enjoy the same status, a couple of opinions crashing the party where, previously, the attendees were fixed inside their pages. No matter if I agree with her comments, or disagree, if I am mystified or unmoved, she never fails to make me think.

Usually I detest the marginal author for being stupid, or bland, or just *wrong*. Even this is a pleasure. Naturally, I assume the superior author would agree with me, were the author able to weigh in, and what's more psychically soothing than siding with an expert? Than coming through opposition on the winning side? But I happen to like the voice in these margins. She is drawn to poetry, underlining the lovely "crunch of leather boots."

On page two she grips her pen and gathers a poem of attention:

If per-
sonality is an unbroken series of successful gestures
hope,   romantic readiness

One senses her readiness entering the world of East Egg, having adopted Nick's savvy as her own. Then Nick pays his first visit to the mansion, and she meets Tom Buchanan.

"Arrogant," she says in response to his gloating, the pen dug deep enough to leave ruts.

On page 13, Tom delivers the confused summary of a book he likes, the gist of which is that whites should prepare for race war.

"Trying to become an intelectual," (sic) she scoffs. "Wants certainties. Doesn't think for himself."

In the margins we can do this, take on the bullies, and tear apart their characters. We are the superior authorities. Pope to the author's creator. Our knees in the groins of the Tom Buchanans of the world.

"Double standard of morals," she writes, when Tom critiques Jordan Baker's meanderings. And when he encourages Daisy's discretion in personal matters, she retorts, "Yet he shows his mistress off to everyone."

At the end of chapter one she washes her hands of the brute, with a cold dismissal:

Tom
Took all the
wind & joy
Out of the lives
Which he met

Who did he represent to her? A first husband? An older brother? A tyrannical father, too early to the grave? Such a damning assessment, and before any real evidence of villainy emerged. Maybe she didn't need evidence. Maybe she knew his type. Maybe she was composing an essay based on the thesis, "Tom Buchanan: Total Asshole."

Whatever it was, after that, she disappears. As

if having suddenly remembered the advice of the father she'd so carefully underscored on page one. She held her tongue in the Valley of Ashes when Tom's corpulent mistress licked her lips, her pitiful husband looking on. And later, when Tom drunkenly breaks her nose in the apartment on West 158th, she says nothing whatsoever about Tom's increasing outbursts of anger, but perhaps that's because he's the victim of duplicity now, and right and wrong seem to be bleeding, and we're all caught up in the quickening gravity of what's coming.

Our marginal author emerges one final time, abruptly, toward the end of the novel on page 133. A prediction of the story's sad conclusion, 30 pages later, when the old dream dies and Gatsby with it, and the Buchanans sell everyone out and slink back west. Her comment is in reference to the row between Gatsby and Buchanan when Daisy admits to having loved them both. She notes decisively and without sentiment:

"Gatsby - inferior."

*the same fucking day,
man.*

My friend Carol lived in the Haight until 1972. She remembers "a bunch of guys doping, loafing, and screwing while the women did all the work." Most of the female boomers I know describe a similarly Grecian milieu, and admit that the sixties, in many ways, were a dark time for women. This is a difficult admission, usually offered up after hours of rapport building and some amount of alcohol. I can only assume reluctance to admit such facts is owed to the overwhelming tide of sixties nostalgia and attendant rhetoric to the contrary. Fear in contradiction, and yes, some confusion in the wake of that tide where they too believed. There is the oft remarked upon tension between the June Cleeverish conservatism transmitted by their mothers and the fist-brandishing feminism of their peers. That feminism, like the attenuated version I inherited, seemed to suggest that promiscuity was the route to liberation. If June was traded for Janis, a pitiful binary masquerading as choice, I confess I prefer the latter, though it seems worth mentioning she (Janis Joplin) capped off her long spree of threesomes with a drug overdose, and died.

Growing up, I played her LP often. Remember the live recording of *Ball and Chain* where she talks about how we have to love today, because tomorrow never happens? I imagine her there, sun-drenched, leather-vested and bead-strung, an aura of frizzy mane, wearing those weird little glasses that don't look good on anyone. How she says, in that quaking, baked-hippie tenor, "It's aaall the same FUCKing day, maaan."

From where I sit, forty years later, this statement rings bitterly true.

My mother, upon whom June's shadow was densely projected, once confided her agonizing attempts to get with the free love program in her early twenties. Attempts which landed her crying outside some party, tipsy, head in hands, after having made a scene when her lover arrived with another girl. The simple fact the ideology disallowed – that sex could *mean* something – to my mother at least. No load of rhetoric from the panamory set could change that. Still, like June, she continued to maintain the status quo, feigning disinterest in monogamy and commitment even after marrying my father. He was a touring musician, and she gave him permission to sleep with other women on tour, so long as he didn't "bring anything home." Which backfired, of course, when, in lieu of an STD, he arrived one day with a different wife.

This, his third marriage, was both monogamous and childless. It's my observation that less the rotating cast of sexual exploits, Casanova desires a mother-type, and the sole position of interest in the life of his lover.

I'm still trying to figure out what the prevailing sexual values were when I was coming of age. I remember at one time thinking that virginity should be saved for someone you love, and that sixteen seemed reasonable. I had friends determined to wait for marriage. I had friends who couldn't wait to *get it over with*, as if their hymens were expired band-aids that needed to be removed. By high school the diversity of views had declined (I attended a small, public, arts magnet: the artistically-inclined children of middle-class hippies). Virginity was a sign of hopeless repression, though obviously some people didn't have much choice in the matter. I once helped my friend Chuck compose a love poem for a girl he wanted to *liberate* while his brother blasted hardcore porn in the next room. Incredible how every metaphor of longing turns depraved with the right soundtrack. I guess it might be true that we had no driving values. That we made it up as we went along. Maybe that's always been the case.

This confused tumult of how we should conduct ourselves in the territories of love and sex came to a head one chilly December Friday during my freshman year of high school. Three older girls I admired took me to see *William Shakespeare's Romeo & Juliet*, a modern interpretation by a shoot-em-up director starring television's Claire Danes and heartthrob Leonardo DiCaprio. We all cried during the mutual suicide scene, then went to the sub shop to smoke cigarettes and swoon over Leo, privately dreaming of our own epic romances which would be arriving any day now. One of the girl's mothers worked nights and wouldn't be home until six the next morning. Even more fortunately for us, this mother had left a gallon bottle of Popov unattended, to which we delivered a respectable blow over the course of that evening's festivities. "Let's play strip poker," the oldest and coolest girl suggested, and we all agreed, though it was clear most of us hadn't quite rounded the bend of puberty yet as we hugged our knees to our meager chests. All but the cool girl, who displayed her full woman's body without shame, chugging the Popov with the verve of a deckhand and commenting on each of our bodies. "I like small boobs," she said in reference to mine, which infused me with enough self-conscious adrenaline to stabilize the spinning room. I don't know if what happened next was spurred by the influence of adult media, or if these *Barely Legal* fans are in fact perving out on real-life possibilities, but one of the girls said, "Who wants to take my virginity?" Then, next thing I knew, they were going at each other on the living room carpet. "Would you like to join us?" asked the cool girl in her smokiest voice. I was stupefied. Not to mention prudish and (even if I hadn't been prostrate on the couch trying not to puke) probably too neurotic to derive any pleasure from the tableau anyhow. I did witness a little of it, between spells of syncope. At some point I remember the cool girl told one of the others, "Your pussy tastes like sugar," and I laughed out loud because *okay, come on, that's so cliché.*

I know it's different in other places. For all its broadcast homogeny America still teems with discrete social groups, each providing its own norms, its own rules for belonging. One friend told me that her husband's cousins in Connecticut were aghast to learn she didn't shave her genitals. "You mean he lets you grow it out?" they shrilled in disgust. "He doesn't *mind?*" Whereas in Portland, the act of a woman shaving her armpits is considered by some groups capitulation to male despotism. Both this friend and I were self-conscious about getting married, worried about being perceived as square or boring. She continues to have difficulty referring to her husband as such (he of the bald pussy kin) and resorts to introducing him by first name only, blushed and stuttering, as if an adulteress caught on the arm of a man she can't account for.

On the other hand, "The engagement rocks on these poor girls' fingers get bigger every term," another friend is distraught to report. She's a feminist studies professor at a notorious liberal arts college and has been tracking The Backslide. "Lisa," she says, utterly depressed. "They're giving up their *names.*"

In Portland, as in Hollywood, marriage has made a comeback and baby bumps are on the rise. It seems every aisle of the natural foods store proffers one of these designer-clad Weebles. And looking at Facebook one gets the sense that these children have been acquired, not to satisfy some deep maternal longing or cultural expectation, but to service the gods of ornamental fashion. Photos of heavily-lacquered young mothers sucking in their cheeks, smashing their best mirror face against the bobblehead of a newborn baby that might as well be a graduation tassel or a bottle of Zima. That said, most of my friends are still single and looking. Like them, I did too much time in the purgatory of Portland dating. An insidious hell of self-important small talk, where one must pretend to care about things like "the blogosphere" and "so-and-so's European tour" and generally behave as if the apocalypse is not nigh. All while fulfilling a series of contradicting expectations: *be sexually open but don't seek your own pleasure, be smart but not threatening, funny but never at the expense of others, reliable and loyal, expect nothing, craft and cook and read great books, be modern but classic, and above all be real and fun. You must always be TONS of fun!* What a bunch of phony-baloney bullshit. I was never good at it. Never understood the rules.

When trying to let a guy down easy I'd wind up awake all night while he picked apart my excuses for breaking up with him, as if therein might lie a loophole to preserve the union: "Okay man, you caught me, I don't *just want to be friends.* Make-up sex?" One guy insisted on staying the night after dissecting my character and, guiltily, I agreed to it. In the morning I rolled over to find him wide awake glaring at me from the wrong side of the bed. "For a minute I thought it was all a bad dream," he hissed.

If I liked a guy, the aloof exterior which first attracted him would dissolve and the frightening visage of a moon-eyed romantic would emerge. I once dated a drummer for a few months about whom I felt ambivalent. Eventually good feelings toward him mounted and I showed up to meet him one day in a plastered smile and dopey longing gaze. He was horrified and broke it off that very night, sat at the edge of the bed shaking his head dismayed and repeating, "I don't get it. You were so *disinterested*."

It should come as no surprise that when this miserable pendulum was finally interrupted by a man with little interest in looking cool, and who said more or less what he meant, I settled down, and rather abruptly. This was met with disbelief and scorn by many of my acquaintances, as if I'd willingly allowed my genitals to be mutilated.

Meanwhile, I bear witness to the agonized script of my single friends.

I met someone. He's ... amazing. We have so much in common. He might be one of the kindest men I've ever met. He's interested in organics. I could see us working on an organic farm someday. We both love crafting. He's incredibly smart, and funny. He's a gentleman. Did I tell you he brought a potted plant instead of flowers to our first date? Isn't that SO awesome? He might even be a bigger feminist than me ... I don't remember the last time I felt this strongly about a person.

I do. It was the last guy. Three months ago. The psychology major who loved little dogs. The so-mature guy. The guy who made you the really romantic mixtape, which was awesome because you still prefer cassettes to CDs. The guy you could see yourself really falling for?

Oh him. He's an asshole and a liar. He never called back or answered my texts. Intimacy issues. I told him he really disappointed me. This guy's totally different than that guy. This guy's one of the most AHMAZING guys I've ever met.

Even more amazing than the guy before last? The graphic designer. The incredibly honest guy. The guy who told you he *really really* liked you but didn't want to move too fast because you were special and he wanted to know you as a friend first and he couldn't stand the thought of hurting or misleading you. The one with the giant prick? Even more than that guy?

Oh ... ya know, I really believe he cared about me. Honestly. I think he's been hurt a lot ... and his feelings for me were just, I don't know, really really intense, so he got scared and backed off before he could get hurt again ... anyway, this new guy's totally different.

To be fair, on the infrequent occasion when a good guy has pursued one of these ladies they are disparaged as "effete" or "needy" or "clingy" and discarded with even less diplomacy. But Lord how I long for the days when a girl's brother and a couple of his buddies could drag assholes like these into the street for a good public ass-whooping. When a girl could grieve her naïveté and perhaps even learn something from it without interference from pop-psychological drivel. At least women like my mother knew the score. Even if they betrayed their true feelings for an ideal, there wasn't this sitcom-thin pretension of a relationship. But who knows. Maybe Portland's new guy really is as amazing as he seems. I mean, he's a feminist and all, and anyway, *Can't you just be happy for me?*

knell of the worried well

October 2010, Shelton, Washington

I'm writing in a cabin in the Olympic woods. The table where I sit most often faces a large picture window, and all day the rain comes down into the forest, dragging dead leaves from the branches. I am occasionally startled by the thud of a Steller's Jay swooping into the window. So far, I haven't made any meaning from this. But I've used these collisions as an excuse to break and walk the cabin's perimeter. Every jay has survived and disappeared into the ferns and I hope this continues to be the case. I am seven days into myself at this artist's house and tired of my mind — of steeping in my own snark and gloomy mood — so I've extended my walk down the gravel road toward town, flanked by dense thickets. The sword ferns are dripping, and the scent of dirt under my boots keeps launching me back in time.

I want to tell you about something I love un-equivocally. Something that, in a way, has already been lost. A place from my childhood, that looked and smelled a lot like this. Lost, my child body leaning over the Nehalem River at dusk, contemplating its rippling curtain. A deeply superstitious part of me balks at the telling for fear of attracting the attention of a petty god. As if the mere mention of joy might mobilize some grand stabilizing force in delivering equal parts misery. An impoverished approach to creation, and a little more about me than I'd like to share, but there it is.

Writing about "nature" is like trying to write about God if you're a believer. Direct statements nearly always sound like lies. If I want to get at the heart of something big, *la condition humaine*, before any rabbi or cancer survivor, I turn to poetry, in part because of what it doesn't say. If I really want inside the mystery I go to the Sufis. The Sufis didn't tackle God head-on but composed love letters that admired specific qualities in their "beloved." When the Sufis say *I have to die for this love / what a bargain*, they're not describing a particular lover but love itself, woven through creation, the final condition of which, of course, is death.

It's a place to start anyway, that river in particular. A place my father took my family when I was a child, 45 miles west of Portland on Highway 26, just before the ocean.

———

The Nehalem River was accessed by one poorly maintained, single-lane gravel road. The turn from the highway was easy to miss. If you hit the Elsie Market you knew you'd gone too far. Our family made the trip annually, sometimes several times in a summer. We piled into Dad's silver Chevy van, and bounced at jarring speeds past the state campground with its toilets and manicured lawn, where the road turned potted as Swiss cheese. In those days, it was possible to drive for hours, to where the river gathered in the bay and poured out into the Pacific, without running across another person. That's all over now. They've brought down half the forest and thrown up manufactured homes, and day and night, even in the off-season, one's brain swarms with the buzz of four-wheelers in the far-off hills. But back then it was quiet in a way that would probably scare me now.

New Yorkers headed for the Hamptons and in the west, we camped. Many families spent the better part of their summers in primitive camp (and by this I mean nowhere maintained by asphalt and day-use fees). My family went out a few times every summer, for as much as a week at a stretch. My father has always been a great lover of the natural world, though he fails to retain any factual information about it, often referring to plants with names he invents on the spot. Names I accepted and recounted as gospel, like "big green" submitted as the proper name for a cedar tree and "blood-berry" for Oregon grape. I eventually relinquished all faith in my father's knowledge of natural science, having been laughed off the playground for claiming that girls' parts were called "deets" and that "VAH-JINE-UH" was the stupidest, most made-up word I ever heard.

Dad had a great enthusiasm for erecting forts and taught me to catch crawdaddies by peeling tiny snails off river rocks (these he called Periwinkles, which may or may not be their name) and tying one to the end of a string, which you dangled in the water until the orange pincher skittered up to your hand. My sister and I made a tidy fortune catching coolers full of crawdads this way, then extorting our parents for the fee of throwing them back. Two dollars a cooler. A better tactic on their part would have been tasking us with cleaning, cooking, and actually consuming the giant bugs, but they were both too emotional for that.

Nehalem is a Salish word meaning *place where people live*, and that's what we did. Casually going about our separate business once the initial camp was raised, like the Swiss Family Robinsons. We'd wake in the mornings, share breakfast, and scatter shortly after. I spent most of my days hunting down my big sister, who would be sun-tanning somewhere, reading Big Bopper. Inevitably rejected, I'd end the afternoon dreaming by the river, watching the great blue herons swoop in, blinking and balancing on their stick legs on the opposite shore. Then dusk would come on and the night birds and the fire crackling in the circle of trees. My mother scooting ground beef around the cast-iron skillet. We'd burn marshmallows while Mom and Dad got blotto on Cold Duck and I'd fight sleep for the chance to stay with them at the fire.

It seems to me now that my love for those trips, for that configuration of my family, for the river as it was, precipitated a certain melancholy. A penchant for cherishing what was — what will never again be — and the depths from which I do it equivalent to my grief. I've gone on in my life to become a grownup, and like most, to suffer. Had I ever any health insurance I'm sure that sentence would have resolved with a nice tight diagnosis: " ... from depression" or " ... from anxiety," likely both. Indigence has spared me that particular mode of dissection, if not the grief itself, which stops by intermittently and latches to my ankles and heavies my steps, and sometimes, if I'm not careful, lunges for my throat. Being in the woods, or the desert, or at the ocean, where the stars might emerge and dwarf my measly concerns, has been therapeutic. Something about feeling small and the absence of abstraction.

A couple of years ago, I suffered a particularly bad episode. I thought I was having heart attacks. What the Emergency Room tech called Pre-emptive Ventricular Constrictions, or PVCs. PVCs are what happen when your heart beats before it has filled with blood, then quickens and beats again to catch up. Sort of like a dancer or athlete after a fall, when they get stuck in a shame loop and lose their rhythm. I was also having difficulty doing anything but staring at the wall, and habitually felt the impulse to shove my head through windows. I blamed it on the weather. The eight months of rain that breed our state's epic beauty. Night and day through the dark winter, commercials for "combating Seasonal Affective Disorder" cycled on my TV screen. That's it, I thought, I must have SAD. And dreamed of sunnier pastures while the sickness crept through the spring and worked on choking me out.

The rain hadn't let up by June and I was feeling desperate, so I decided I'd drive out to the desert of southeastern Oregon, where the stars are visible at night and you hear coyotes laughing over their kills. I packed up my car with a tent and blankets, a jug of water and a few granola bars and drove eight hours past the rain cloud into the hot and sunny June of

Winnemucca, singing along to Bob Dylan B-sides and feeling better already. I opened a cattle gate and took a BLM road into the hills. In the insect-humming noon, coarse sage exploded from the earth all around. I spied a little clearing at the top of a hill and decided to make it my spot. Slamming the car door the sage-brush rustled and I could hear the bodies of rattlers winding away.

My plan was to sit on a hill and think, and ask a few questions of my own, "What the fuck?" being chief among them. I did it for three days. Just sat there without moving, without eating food or drinking water. What some people call a vision quest. I prefer to call it sitting. Whatever you call it, the point has always been to die, approximately. The ritualized death of the old self, and the birth of a new dream. Some have observed that hallucination is a consequence of starvation and dehydration, a fine point. I can only speak for myself. What happened to me on the hill those few days and nights was so far outside my body, that the suggestion I might just have been *trippin'* strikes me as more quaint than mocking. I saw and heard some weird stuff up there, to be sure, but in the end the most profound experience was also the most expected: longing for water. It was the first time in my life I'd been truly thirsty. The best way to understand the feeling is to imagine your first love, and the kind of obsessive whole body attention you helplessly gave every detail of that person, real or imagined. And how a scrap of some song piping through a mall, or the faintest whiff of their shampoo could send your being skidding into rumination. If you can, imagine the absolute height of your longing for that loved one.

I was in love with water. No life without the god of water. I shoved my nose into the desert floor and dug my fingernails in the dirt, down until I located a premonition of moisture, and dragged my nostrils against it, greedily sucking up the scent. I wept without tears and apologized to the world for all my ungratefulness. That smell cast my mind back to the Nehalem River. All that time as a child spent staring into water came flooding into me. I wanted inside it again. To see it and smell it and savor it. Lying there in my dirty face and dreaming of rain, all other cities and states, all other possible existences, were obliterated.

I still drive out that gravel road just before the Elsie Market, though I know what I'm looking for is gone. The river has shifted and filled with silt, runoff from the shrubby, clear-cut hills — and anyway, I'm not the same. My mind is infected with worry, no matter how I try to still it and see the water bugs lifting out of the mud in the oblique afternoon sun.

My sister has children of her own now, whose faces are burned blue in my memory by the light of Game Boy screens. And miles away my father is growing old, though he still takes them into the woods when they come for a visit, to build forts and play again like brothers, like boys.

A *place where people live*, but can a place live in a person after it's destroyed? Nehalem, I carry your big greens and crawdads with me. Your great blue herons and rocky banks. Hard work keeping the clear-cut at bay inside my own being, but what a bargain.

the body autumnal

a story

Like anything, it begins with a collision. Two hours south of Portland, Oregon, in the belly of that tar-black leviathan, I-5. Spring has been quietly replaced by a heat that draws reflective mirages from the empty road ahead. Lewis and Clark loom from a 3-D painting on a roadside historical marker, the only point of interest for twenty miles. Their gaze is of hope and invention and falls on a gas station where a van and its human contents have stalled.

A young man crouches outside the station store, smoking a B&H and eyeing the attendant. He spits at his feet between drags. The attendant waves a slip of paper at the boy and the boy nods, stubs his cigarette in the pool of saliva and follows him inside. A minute later he's adjusting the rearview and shifting his butt in the plastic bucket seat. He considers a sandwich, a bath, and turns the key. Empty Coke cans, small collections of ash and torn-open cigarette packs litter the unoccupied passenger seat. The boy lifts two fingers at the attendant as he pulls away but the man does not see.

Soon the highway has collected a steady stream of cars. The day has stretched into a flat heat, the sun drawn to half-mast. He's thick in thought. When the steering fails the boy wakes from his stupor and looks wildly around. He pulls on the wheel firmly, first right, then left, and curses. It won't work. He pulls again both right and left, and makes an awful sound, a caged sound. It's no use. He's moving too fast. The van glides into the right lane smoothly, clipping a Camry at the nose.

"Shit," he says, as if to rescue his heavy body from sleep, and grabs back hold of the wheel, attempts the frantic correction.

In a trance, other drivers fix on the vehicle's swerving and pull onto the shoulder. A collective gasp as the van flips onto the median, sending clumps of earth and grass soaring above. Each subsequent flip incites a scream, a turning away. They are circus-goers taking on spectacle, its swollen physical comedy. The van and the earth are drawn together magnetically, the bounce, the repulsion. The spectators gather together, already deep in the meaning of it.

The scene of the crash plays as Miss Eva Stark prepares for sleep. In the anxious dark of her bedroom, in the heat of the bed and her tossing, other corpses parade under her eyelids but his is largest. His obstructs the center, cracks in the legs and the ribs and folds over itself backward. She calls "Charles" to the dark of her room and "Charles" to that other place.

He didn't die in the road. He was wheeled to a white room made appropriate for dying. It goes on and on like this automatically.

THE FUNERAL

Eva is tired at the funeral. She does not slow for not sleeping; she quickens. Her heart speeds and her fingers won't stop moving. The cadaver in its box is like a metal rod, cold and conductive. She joins her hand with the iron pew of his palm while the funeral director watches from the corner, calm as a ceramic saint. Charles is bloated, at least ten pounds richer in liquid. Not calm, exactly. More like ever-so-slightly surprised. *You're dead*, thinks Eva. *Never again*, she thinks, and imagines ribs exploding from the torso, moaning, rolling on the concrete, pleading for his mother or *help, God,* or just *please*. At first he reminds her of wax, but it's worse than that; inside he is steel. In a single moment he draws the last of her heat.

His family home is in a suburb of Portland, a large house on a trimmed lawn. People meet there after the funeral to drink among his things. His books fit on a single shelf and bear titles seemingly unrelated to one another, the library of a young man who didn't have enough time to develop his taste. His old punk records lean against the foot of the bed. There's a photo of him at the airport in a white t-shirt and Hawaiian-print tie, wearing huge plastic sunglasses and a look of supreme boredom.

The objects make her a stranger. They knew him better.

Eva Stark drinks whiskey. Tells a newspaperman in khaki pants that Charles was a guy who could talk the shirt off your back. Someone else tells a story about Charles double-fisting forties and driving at high speeds through the hills. It is meant to be funny. Spectacular, funny stories all around. Briefly, she considers grabbing someone by the throat.

Now here comes Collier.

DOCTOR COLLIER: Is that whiskey you're drinking?

EVA: I'm at a wake.

DOCTOR COLLIER: If you say so.

EVA: I want out of here.

DOCTOR COLLIER: I'm not much for funerals to be honest.

EVA: Is anyone?

DOCTOR COLLIER: You'd be surprised.

EVA: I doubt it.

DOCTOR COLLIER: I'm disturbed by hunting trophies. Just look at that poor deer, forever frozen in headlights.

EVA: His only kill.

DOCTOR COLLIER: Their kitchen, on the other hand — we installed a similar island recently, only ours boasts a genuine granite top. What do you suppose that is? Formica?

EVA: Do you know why I first came to you?

DOCTOR COLLIER: Your mother arranged it.

EVA: Do you or don't you?

DOCTOR COLLIER: I know why. Do you?

EVA: Things in my head.

DOCTOR COLLIER: Invisible suggestions.

EVA: I wanted you to tell me something.

DOCTOR COLLIER: Yes.

EVA: Something true.

In the weeks after, she pursues Charles through the wreck, lusting after every gory detail provided in witness statements or the coroner's report. She can't sleep. It's her ribs. No matter how she arranges herself, any moment they might break through as easily as a tooth. To kill the sensation she tries to remember him as he was before. All in one piece. In his bedroom, propped on his bed, a few pillows lodged just below the shoulders, knees up, thighs resting immodestly open. In those faded black jeans, no belt. The old white t-shirt, the one with the coffee stain, riding up, revealing an inch of hairy stomach just below his navel. He lifts his head from the pillow and picks the guitar.

In the end, the memory perverts. The sheet runs red or the guitar twists into a hunk of metal and cuts him.

DOCTOR COLLIER: The mind is tricky. You can't always trust it.

EVA: You're the shrink.

DOCTOR COLLIER: Trauma forms pathways in the brain, chemical imbalances that distort our perceptions.

EVA: What do you suggest?

DOCTOR COLLIER: When an ugly thought comes around, take a deep breath and replace it with a pleasant one. I use my vacation home on Whidbey Island.

EVA: What if your vacation home went up in flames?

DOCTOR COLLIER: I suppose I see what you mean.

EVA: Some things can't be ignored.

DOCTOR COLLIER: We have medications for that.

In a window display on West Burnside someone has strung up a photo of Charles in a gaudy heart-shaped frame. The caligraphy demands that he rest in peace. Eva comes by to see him out in the open.

Outside the glass cube mill adults with plans, the fixed cycle of seasons in which he is no longer allowed to participate. Eva says, "It's not like I don't live in a box," and lights a cigarette. She reads, in a neon pink frame, *Local boy, 20, dies in crash*, and tells herself he suffered, and scrunches up her face. Traffic inches up the hill and into the woods, where they grew together from children to adults. At the top of the hill, among a thousand others, he decays.

BOXES

That summer, Eva Stark walks around town wanting to get fucked. It's cold and automatic, having little to do with desire and much to do with a desire to be dismembered. She wants to be torn in half.

Her willingness does not go unnoticed. In bars, chilly conversations leap suddenly to propositions. Her cause is injured by her bluntness and leaves many initially horny men with a limp one and a paternal concern for her wellbeing. At 2 a.m., she sulks home alone in the transitional night. Passing storefronts she observes her face, its tendency to twist and unwring itself and twist again, the way a man might stare at his flexing bicep. She's a stranger in her house, its six rooms, everything hardwood and draft. She enters it only to sleep. Late at night, she weaves unseen through the neighborhood. All the old neighbors who've moved away or hidden in their houses have forgotten her, but she has not forgotten them. The old life projects from their windows as she passes. On the lawn, transparencies of their children run through sprinklers. They take one another by the hand and face her.

Eva has had the upstairs loft ever since her father moved away. A few years ago, she discovered that she could lie on her floor eight times over, wall to wall. That is to say, if she'd had any friends, and they were roughly her size, they could form a line of eight lying flat on their backs, head to toe, from one wall to the other. She's tested the figure many times. Sometimes it's eight and sometimes it's nine. Out of one hundred counts, ninety-seven amounted to eight.

But she hasn't been up there in a year, opting instead for the plaid couch in the living room across from the little TV. The big TV was sold at an auction along with most of the furniture. Good riddance. The little TV with the rabbit ears used to show her He-Man and Gummi Bears. Its light repels bad thoughts.

DOC COLLIER: Ever consider hiring a maid?

EVA: Funny.

DOC COLLIER: I am perfectly serious. We pay just $45 a visit for Brenda. She is very thorough. I'll give you her number if you'd like.

EVA: No thanks.

DOC COLLIER: A little lonely around here.

EVA: Not any more than before.

DOC COLLIER: You seem to be running some kind of an experiment. All this empty space ... reminds me of something. Does it remind you of something?

EVA: Probably not.

DOC COLLIER: It reminds me of a little boy we used to discuss. What was his name? The boy from the experiment?

EVA: You know his name.

DOC COLLIER: Oh yes. You certainly did fret for Caspar. How's the old ankle chain? Any eyes come out of the dark recently?

EVA: Nope.

DOC COLLIER: Progress!

She lies on her side in last night's clothes, their sweat and smoke informing her sleep. One arm draws her knees to her chest, the other falls limp over the couch's edge in a dead reach.

Not fucked but still drunk, Eva rides a bottle off to work. Days melt together, the sun never fully sets or rises. There is a sleeping box, a working box, and a box that moves between. Every day, the ten-minute walk to the train along the shortest route, crossing when possible in diagonals, the same fat woman walking the same fat dogs, the houses cramped in rows. Some stinky lady riding the train until her nod wears off. Sometimes there's a stranger who wants to talk, or eat her alive, or touch her under her clothes.

She makes fists and shifts in the hard plastic seat. Imagines the street cracked like an egg, exposing the molten yolk of the earth, against which the cars appear in their peaceful plummet small as salt crystals.

Don't think it.

The brain is an asshole, it is an engine begging to be derailed.

THE CAFÉ

Linda comes into the café with Cathy and the tall junkie guy. They're all junkies, but he looks extra bad: jaw hung open like a hooked fish, stringy hair falling out in places, graying in others. He's on his ankles like a sloppy stilt-walker, beginning each step at the quadricep, his leg reaching a right angle before he sets it down again. Like the sneaky walk villains use in silent movies.

Linda hides it pretty well except for the distended stomach. If she weren't fifty she could pass for pregnant. And poor Cathy, who began coming to the café just a year ago, a normal, healthy woman. Pretty cogent as far as anyone could tell, holding down a job in hosiery at Nordstrom. She now mistakes coffee beans on the counter for raisins and falls asleep standing up or lights cigarettes in the middle of the dining room while waiting for her drink.

The café is next to the bus mall and one floor down from the methadone clinic, so it isn't uncommon for junkies to become regulars. People were trading pills there until the cops started hanging out from 10 a.m. to 6 p.m.

"Don't you pigs ever fucking leave?" Linda complains. "Shouldn't you go blow my tax money on something?"

"Yeah, go blow it on blow!" says the wobbly guy.

He and Linda double over in hysterics.

"Or, go ..." she sniggers, "blow it on a *blow job*!"

Overcome, Linda and Wobbles sag into a pile on the floor. The cops cuff them right there and drag them through the café out the door, the two of them hooting and hollering the whole time. "Yee-Haw! Yip-yip-Yoo!"

If crazy were determined by decibels alone, Linda and Wobbles would be hands-down shithouse. But it's Cathy who disturbs Eva most. She's lost her mind in less than a year. That means that anyone can. Eva fears that she will be sucked from her body into Cathy's if eye contact is maintained. That she'll become prisoner in that body but stay in her own mind. This is another thought keeping her awake.

COLLIER: Is this the one where you get sucked into the body of a stray dog?

EVA: It never actually happens. I worry that it will.

COLLIER: That's preposterous.

EVA: Thanks.

COLLIER: What's the other one then?

EVA: Crazy people ... and the big fish with the whiskers stuck in a tiny tank at some bourgeois sushi hell-hole.

COLLIER: Do you know what all of this reminds me of?

EVA: I can guess.

COLLIER: Caspar and the ankle chain.

Caspar And The Ankle Chain

Anton Phelps, a psychologist specializing in early childhood development, explored attachment using his own son as subject. His hope was to create a controlled environment that excluded systems of reward.

COLLIER: No gifts. No verbal reinforcements.

EVA: No touch affirmation.

COLLIER: That the boy would develop unencumbered by social expectations —

EVA: — perhaps the true, unpolluted nature of man would become evident through his boy!

COLLIER: That's the spirit. Donahue did a story, if I remember correctly. By the end of the program the whole audience hated my profession. As one woman with very large bangs put it, "Psychologists are psychotics!"

EVA: Mr. Babcock taught a unit on the Phelps study in seventh grade. That's when it started.

COLLIER: Thank you, Mr. Babcock.

EVA: The boy met the diagnostic criteria for schizophrenia by the end of his fifth year.

COLLIER: Highly unusual. Phelps concluded that the desire to be among other humans was a core trait of our kind, to the extent that, when denied the resources to meet that need —

EVA: A subject will hallucinate or willfully invent companions in order to meet it. Side effects of the experiment included: heart arrhythmia, anxiety, night terrors, self-injury, and a nearly fatal cardiac arrest at age seven, treated at Saint Vincent's Hospital. The hospital alerted Child Protective Services and they removed the boy from his home for neglect.

He'd been kept in the cellar, leg locked to the radiator. Skin covered in sores, loss of sensation in the feet, and a heart too animate for its valves. On days when he was to be left completely alone, Phelps on his way to a mysterious clinic, the heart would nearly clear its cave. After the crunch of the lock, the withdrawal of the doctor's many keys, when his steps had shrunk to silence and the whir of the car engine gone off into space, eyes came out of the dark. From the far back corner of the cellar they came, eyes unblinking and unmoored. When the women came with their badges and papers a great buzzing filled the darkness. One of the ladies wept when she saw him. The other looked like she could bite through metal. Neither noticed the eyes swarming in the corner. Caspar would have turned from them too if not for the burning light in the open door. A piece of the world he would soon inhabit, had longed to enter, but could not yet painlessly face.

COLLIER: Poetry?

EVA: Salvation.

COLLIER: So they say.

They lifted him easily into the outside air and without knowing it, took all those eyes with him. They swarmed right out of the cellar with their little unblinking lights and trailed like streamers behind him. They seemed more benign by daylight, friendly even. When he was so alone, awake in some stranger's house, they'd come to him like a mother. Haloing the heads of his foster parents or stuck among the popcorn in his ceiling like stars.

COLLIER: Careful there.

Caspar began with a man and his vision. Three million years of human history beneath the doctor's heel. Lucky for us, the old stories hide underground where the heel can't reach, and it's only a matter of time before they find a way out.

DEFENESTRATION

The end of the same day lives in a bar. A neat whiskey and an Oly stubby for starters. Not alone, playing footsie with a barstool, spine hooked into a drink like a scythe, scanning the room to pin a sap sad enough to talk. Because Eva Stark is pretty for now. Black dye hides her mousy brown roots. Black pencil distracts predators from the pale exposure of her eyes. An old blue dress hangs loose on the doll body, ever titless.

There are four or five others who can be counted on for a drink at least two nights a week. All in their twenties, and all with big plans and big college graduate words to back those plans. They remind her that these are her young days. They remind her to have fun while she can, but every time Eva makes it to the bathroom to scrutinize the mirror (and considers putting her head through it, derailing the engine), it becomes painfully evident that no one is having any fun anymore.

COLLIER: That is some red lipstick.

EVA: It goes.

COLLIER: Having fun tonight?

EVA: Miserable.

COLLIER: It's called defenestration. The throwing of a person or thing out of a window.

EVA: What's it called when the person you're throwing is you? Or just your head? And actually, it's not *throwing* so much as it's forcing or putting through.

COLLIER: I'll work on it.

EVA: Good. I'd like to give it a name.

Portland's an alcoholic these days. The bars outnumber the trees. Bars with icy names like

HEAVEN or AURORA. Bars that feel like hospital rooms, on spaceships, gusting through the cold cosmos at drunken speeds. Everyone's a drunk. It's what no one likes to talk about. Even the local alternative weekly, with its sad attempts at investigative journalism, has avoided the subject but for an annual ten page color spread addressing the five W's of drinking. In Eva's case the Why is amorphous and the rest is unimportant, especially the Who. If no company comes there are points of fixation to bridge the ugly depth between drunk and unconscious. More recently she has chosen to fixate on Charles. He's on the bed with the hunk of metal.

Collier suggests that when she feels overwhelmed by fixation she should name it and write it a letter. She's written thousands. Letters to No Life After Death, to Going Crazy, to Tumors.

Dear Dad,

    The look of your face in my face is troubling.

Eva

Before her father left them and her mother eschewed religion in favor of Dr. Collier's drugs, they had a pastor. Eva's episodes led the family to him. "A violation of God's law has caused this," he counseled. "Try reading the bible at night for comfort. Avoid Job and Revelations." But as soon as they'd begun the bible ritual Eva's head filled up with the sentence, "I love Satan."

No I DON'T, she'd say.

"I love Satan."

NO NO NO, I love God, I love Jesus, Jesus is my savior, God is my father ...

"I love Satan."

As an adult, she can't think of it except when drunk for fear of manifesting an attack. Given enough focus (especially focus backed by dread or, she supposes, even love, though it has not been her experience) anything can come forth from the void. Tumors, paralysis, Satan himself. It might also be possible to manifest love, or money, or, probably, walking on water if the nasty voices weren't so strong. Always pushing her intent clean out of her head.

EVA: It's not my fault I'm this way, you know?

COLLIER: I know.

EVA: Some people call it a gift.

COLLIER: The Lipin Apaches believed that people with mental retardation were touched by the gods.

EVA: Who says they aren't?

COLLIER: Sometimes inclusion requires deifi-cation.

EVA: Don't be an asshole.

CASPAR

Caspar doesn't drink and Caspar doesn't dwell. If there is a hungry mouth he puts something beautiful in it. If things get desperate, he uproots his hair or cuts out a square of his arm. Every leaf, every grass blade seems to lift in chorus with his passing — *Do that for which you are made!* It's summertime. People like to go swimming and walk together and not just stew around inside among the negatively charged ions and microorganisms. It makes sense that Caspar should also. If he were one of his own dead, he would be angry to find a shimmering-fleshed man in the middle of a limited and mortal paradise, whining and generally unappreciative of his life. It wouldn't be a nice gesture at all.

But for what was I made? he wonders aloud. A scrap of sound caught by a pair of passing ladies, their arms weighted by department store shopping bags, who draw into themselves upon hearing him speak, not commenting to one another until he is certainly out of earshot. One of the ladies murmurs that it's a shame. "It is a shame that such a fine looking young man has lost his mind." How much he resembles her brother Bernard, she thinks, Bernard having been tall and black-haired in his youth and who now lies collecting bedsores at the state hospital, demented. If given the chance to comment, Caspar would tell her that Bernard has replaced a piece of his mind with something more useful: the ability to converse with those who will call for him on the opposite shore of the great dark waters.

The quiet look between the ladies, its mild fear and its remembrance of Bernard, does not wound Caspar. Their tendency to elide the certainty of their own demise is childlike and sweet. In his heart, he wishes them well and continues on along the water and over bridges, falling in love with everyone. His head hung out on his neck like a paddle ball, sporting a sideways grin. Rubber armed and rubber legged, waving to nothing in particular. God and Earth and all of Caspar's dead know he is good.

CASPAR'S COURTSHIP

All over the city, people unwrap their cocoons and meet one another in the flesh. In the park on the river they share blankets. They look at one another and speak with intensity, but poor Caspar is alone. He wants to court a young woman and has begun viewing romantic films at the cineplex and reading poems in order to learn how to speak effectively to her. The movies suggest that he could not attempt conversation without first maintaining a kind of wardrobe. Caspar has decided to base his costume on something the girl at the coffee shop might find appealing. One day he spots her entering a used clothing store and follows her in.

The girl attending the dressing room suggests a pair of old jeans that are far too tight, in Caspar's opinion, a worn black T-shirt, and some starred sneakers. He accepts her advice and thanks her for her time.

VIOLET

She tried it a few times before, Eva's mother. First time by sucking on the end of the revolver her husband had left for protection. After five minutes of tearful slobbering she removed the barrel from her mouth. Eva found her asleep in the cleaning closet wearing her blue flannel jammies with a gun in her hand. The next day Eva's mother drove over the hill into the suburbs where her husband lived with his new wife and unloaded six bullets into their shiny black Cobra.

"You can keep it, asshole!" she yelled and chucked the empty gun at the car.

Dr. Collier said her unhealthy actions symbolized a healthy desire to move on from the divorce.

Eva was staying with her father the second time it happened. She'd moved in with him her sophomore year of high school to be closer to Charles and to dodge the city school where she lived up to her whispered family epithet, "Stark staring mad." Her mother, Violet, had been spending more and more time on the couch. With the TV on or off, a book in hand or none, she just lay there. In her father's home, Eva learned to enter with ease, without fear of a screaming woman. Or worse, silence.

EVA: You should have known better.

COLLIER: Me? I assumed that she was taking her medication as prescribed.

EVA: I shouldn't have left her.

COLLIER: You must keep in mind, Eva ... you're not the only one in the world who's lost something.

EVA: Nobody else acts like they have.

COLLIER: Don't be dramatic.

EVA: I can't even go near the beach now. It makes me want to throw up.

COLLIER: You might try the San Juan islands. Last summer the family vacationed on Whidbey. It was marvelous.

That year, in the last week of August, they found her. The old couple who owned The Little Bee Motel at Seaside discovered her passed out on the floor of one of their rooms in a pool of vomit, using her own arm for a pillow. The empty pill bottle sat, obvious as a stage prop, in the center of the table. The fan sliced its dull revolution overhead. An EMT told Eva that it was lucky her mother had rolled on her side, otherwise she would have asphyxiated.

Luck is dangerous that way. Everyone knows the third time's the charm.

THE BEACH

At the café the circus is in full effect. Linda continues to exclaim that she's nobody's patsy, picking the skin from her fingertips and chewing her nails as Cathy works the child lock on her lighter.

Dear Linda and Cathy,

Please refrain from infecting me with your sickness.

Eva Stark

A gangly scenester guy in too-big Chuck Taylors comes in, apparently unaffected by the drug-induced theatrics surrounding. His eyes are large and buggy. His skin so taut on his cheekbones any variation in expression appears to be painful. He stands at the counter a long while, lost in choices, before finally ordering at a barely audible level, a cappuccino.

Eva is irritated. It's not just the fumbling introverts that bother her. She's equally disgusted by customers who muck up the process with too many words. She doses the Portafilter and tamps. There is always some sad jerk who will stand at the counter long after his allotted time has expired, prattling on about his favorite new band, movie, etc. She pours the milk into the pitcher and steams. Doesn't matter how long the line behind him is, it could be wrapped around the block and he'd still find it entirely appropriate to ask her if she likes music. What the hell kind of a question is that? *Nope. Don't like music. But if you want to hang out some time in vacuous silence I guess that'd be cool.*

The gangly stranger reminds her of an alien, only with good bone structure and clear skin. Like an alien come to earth masquerading as an attractive man. Her hand considers reaching to pull at his skin mask but decides against it. She sets his drink in front of him and asks, "Hemingway, huh?"

The alien looks at her. At her neck, to be precise.

"Hmm ..." he says, turning his book over in his hands as if it had miraculously appeared out of thin air. Looks at the book and then to Eva, from deep in the sockets of those unblinking eyes.

EVA: Does everyone have to have some fucking affectation?

COLLIER: Why so hostile?

EVA: All I'm saying is that I wish people would just be normal.

COLLIER: I bet you do.

EVA: Fuck you, Doc.

COLLIER: Eva Stark. If you cannot control your anger I will terminate this arrangement.

EVA: I'm sorry. God. I'm wound up.

COLLIER: You might consider a yoga class. My wife's demeanor has improved greatly since she's taken it up. She has us on an Ayurvedic diet that is just wonderful. I have so much more energy.

Eva has experienced only one moment of insoluble rapture. On the beach, when she was seventeen. Under the stars, dumb with awe but loved in total, it seemed by virtue of her breath and pulse alone. She was with Charles there, who kissed with the kind of seriousness that aches. Who shot her full of stars, their magnets still in her cells on hot nights as she climbs the hill to his headstone. He who remains as strange as any man, even in death.

COLLIER: Not the beach.

EVA: Let me have it.

They'd gone for a friend's birthday, somebody's uncle had a house. Most everyone was on acid, but Eva and Charles had abstained. One of them had to drive back for work the next day. There was a bonfire between two large dunes which everyone sat around, drinking and talking too loud. It made her nervous, not just the prospect of cops but the way it didn't fit. Too much yelling. She couldn't stand it. The louder they spoke the tighter her jaw, the heavier the pressure in her ears, and soon it felt like a million fists had drawn back inside her body. She fantasized running them off with a flaming stick but couldn't summon the nerve and so escaped down the dune toward the water.

Charles followed.

EVA: He kissed me.

COLLIER: Huh.

EVA: I didn't know he wanted to.

COLLIER: It's all very romantic, the sand and the moon and all that.

But the nerve of that night died in the root, run off by the prospect of empathy. The deep common matter of which men are made. Eva can no longer speak to them. Cannot possibly survive the crush of their hopes. Their vulnerabilities.

COLLIER: It's not all that bad, really.

Take the alien guy in her periphery, with his big shoes and his tight jeans and a fist in his throat. She'd like to put a pillow to his face.

COLLIER: Say, did you know that the fates spin three threads into the cord of destiny?

EVA: Do tell.

COLLIER: Thought, will, and action.

Eva grabs a bleach rag and wipes the counter in fervent circles, hot-faced and head-bowed. She tucks her face into her shoulder to block the alien's stare.

COLLIER: Do you ever have the sensation that somehow your cord's been cut?

EVA: What do you mean?

COLLIER: Do you love Satan, Eva?

EVA: What the fuck is this?

At table six, Cathy lights a cigarette and kisses Linda on the cheek. Eva waddles toward them as if on the deck of a ship. Landless grey rolling on all sides.

COLLIER: Would you like me to show you hell? It's a wonderful sort of cocktail party.

EVA: I'm not listening.

COLLIER: The fates wear mini-skirts and leg warmers. They snort halos from their reflections.

EVA: Shut up.

COLLIER: One of them carries a razor blade. She'll cut the cord as it's woven for no reason whatsoever.

EVA: That's not true.

COLLIER: Oh yes. I'm afraid there's just no meaning in it.

Linda prances around Cathy's chair, clapping her hands, begging for a cigarette. Mid-revolution she crashes into Eva, pulling them both to the floor. Eva struggles to avoid her eyes.

COLLIER: Look at this woman. Her life is for *nothing*. When her liver kaputs or some boyfriend shoots her, that will be for nothing, too.

Eva pulls herself to her feet, shaking. Plucks the cigarette from Cathy's hand and pokes it into her own mouth.

"Hey ..." Cathy protests. "That's my cigarette."

COLLIER: The line is fraying.

Eva drags.

COLLIER: At any moment it will snap.

NEW YEAR

Charles had a problem with his mind. He'd get stuck in the husk of it. Had you met the two of them together, Charles and Eva, when they were seventeen, smoking cigarettes in front of Pizza Hut or shoulder tapping at 7-11, you would never have guessed they shared even one uniting characteristic. Charles was self-contained and quiet. He possessed an indiscriminate calm, whether ordering chicken nuggets, discovering he'd misplaced his weed, or being told that he was loved. Even when he laughed he rarely gave in to the kind of explosive, piss-yourself cackling of most teenagers. Instead, a tiny smile would crease the corners of his mouth, and a nearly imperceptible chuckle from deep in his body would ever-so-slightly shake his shoulders.

Eva was a loudmouth. Fond of inciting fights, talking shit to JNCO punks and flipping off cops, only to step out of the line of fire when hell broke loose, claiming that free verbalization was integral to her therapy. She often warned Charles that if he could not express himself properly she would have to help him do so. She was always rooting around for loose threads to tug at. When angered, she maintained the sense of being outside of her body, would watch her physical face contort and sound out frenzied complaints from a satellite of calm. While she was somewhere at her root removed, Charles was still of the body and a storm inside.

New Year's Eve 1998 at the cabin on Mt. Hood (the whole extended family locked in with him, taken hostage by the snow and the dark) he busted his husk. Spent the night pacing the upstairs bedroom after a frustrating conversation with an uncle about child exploitation in China. Eva caught a scrap of it through the door. Apparently his uncle would not accept that the institution of compulsory education was, in essence, the American equivalent of Nazi concentration camps. An only slightly flawed analogy, she'd thought at the time.

After two hours of their back and forth, Charles's poor uncle grew weary. He could smell the roast reaching completion in the kitchen below and hear the bottles uncorking. Despite Charles's accusations of defeat, the uncle excused himself with a sad sigh.

Eva, hidden behind the door at his exit, returned just in time to watch Charles hit one of the cedar beams with his fist and collapse.

He sat in the center of the room, hugging his knees, emitting low groans wrung from his stomach. And then, as suddenly as it had begun, the sobbing ceased. He stood up and looked at his feet for a long time.

COLLIER: Did you go to him then?

EVA: Something stopped me.

COLLIER: The fragrance of danger.

He hauled off and punched the cedar beam. It didn't make much noise but you could tell the impact had traveled into his shoulder because he stood rubbing it for a minute. Then he hauled off and punched the beam again and again and again.

His mother called for him to come down to eat but he didn't hear, or perhaps, heard perfectly well and that was what moved him to the window. Eva grew sick then, when he went to the window and drew back his bloody nub.

EVA: I could have stopped him.

COLLIER: But you didn't.

The shatter, the crisp ring of glass popping, the thousand irreconcilable mirrors. His blood and commotion below, the family stampeding upstairs, where he stood screaming in the open window, "You're all rapists!"

COLLIER: Back to the beach.

EVA: I don't want to.

COLLIER: Nonsense. It is a perfect evening. You've just made love beneath a ceiling of stars. What are you thinking about?

After his climax, his release and rolling off of her, she began to pick ever so gently at him. The questions presented themselves innocently enough, "What are you thinking about?" or "You don't regret it do you?" but inside they were screaming, "What have you done with me?"

He lay with his hands folded unnaturally on his chest, eyeing the dark sky. And then, suddenly, grabbed his T-shirt with a start and took off down the beach away from where she reeled, partially undressed and sick.

COLLIER: How did you feel then?

EVA: Like shit. Obviously.

She'd tugged on her clothes and pursued his darkening body, hysterically, first at a jog and then at an all-out run. She planned to tell him something, but once she'd caught up, before the first words came tumbling to the mouth, he grabbed her with hate in his face and threw her to the sand. *You fucking bitch.*

EVA: It was wrong.

COLLIER: I don't know.

EVA: It was all fucked up.

COLLIER: It was the plain fact of two people acting. Actions are actions. People are neither good nor evil.

EVA: They are claustrophobic and cruel, always walking into some dark expanse without you.

COLLIER: It seems we agree.

AUTUMNAL

The trees have relinquished their green, their abundance, in a sudden pivot toward conservation. The sap of all living things retracts, putrefying fruits, pulsing in the stalks. The proof of death burns red, ignites from the edge of each shrinking vein and makes paper of skin. There is the sentiment of fists beating the interior of a locked trunk, help-cries pickled in carbon dioxide. The tidal flailings of all God's creatures broken on the shorelines of their pride. Pride quiets them. They burn and unloose from the life-branch, join a composting tumult. The decaying season and its blunt assertion of ends will not be avoided by any of them.

Caspar loves all of it. He picks tragedy and miracle apart with his hands. He peels its sections from stem until his fingers stain red and orange and a man comes from the house saying, "Get off my goddamned lawn!"

His feet burst up, then out. They perform a strange little song and dance in tandem. The street is neither flat nor stationary beneath him. Rather, he climbs, foot-over-foot as the earth lifts its many helpful hands to meet him. All the way to the river.

O, the romance of the river. Standing at Waterfront Park in a backpack, stroking the metal girder, gauging your courage. The odor of concealed deeds. The violent forcing apart of legs. The sacked body, just cold, tumbling unattended down the bank. Or the mutter of a certain section, knowing it will never be met again. The comfort of its repetition. The heartbreak of its repetition. The words spoken aloud there, never to be retrieved. A story about how to die.

There are stories about how to live, but they hide underground. Long before the heavy lattice of city streets, the amnesia-inducing speed, the fires rushed under a banner of progress that made corpses of the people who lived here first. Gutted, shot full of holes, left to rot under the eye of the weeping sun. The civilized world arrived burning and the old world ran, skin in flames, leaving tracks of charred flesh on the surface of the land that they loved. Through their torn skin the stories evacuated, got underground. Sometimes, folks living under bridges absorb them. They speak in codes not immediately accessible to house dwellers. Most people wouldn't guess, while making their morning commute, that the stinky lady on the train, riding her nod off, holds within her body a story to make sense of their gaping holes.

A VISIT TO DOCTOR COLLIER

"Well," he smiles, "come on in."

A girl not much older than Eva sits behind Mrs. Parr's desk, bent over some papers with a pen in her hand. Her hair is slicked back in a tight blonde pony-tail. She wears a turquoise-blue pant suit that causes her to resemble a kind of severe, Aryan amphibian. "Hello!" she says brightly, clicking her pen.

"Mrs. Parr retired in the spring. Sarah here is her granddaughter. She's just completed her MSW at Columbia."

Dr. Collier smiles lovingly at Sarah and Sarah reciprocates. Neither of them speak. Eva turns for the door.

"Now, wait a second," says Collier, grabbing her arm. "Let's just go in my office for a chat." He wraps his arm around her shoulder and leads her down the hall. "You remember my office, don't you?"

It's the same carpet. Blue and yellow diamonds. The wall hanging is new, a waterfall in a mossy wood and underneath, in cursive letters, the word *Inspiration*.

"That wall hanging is new," she says.

"So, catch me up." Collier swivels in his chair. His face is large, unavoidable. "How's the house?"

"It's fine. I've decided to stay."

"Good."

"My uncle has been handling the financials."

"Good. Good."

Collier looks to the picture of the waterfall, probably relieved that his children are normal and well-adjusted. In the photo on his desk, taken last summer in the San Juan islands, they wear khaki shorts and polo shirts. The children share his smug smile and pug nose. It's their uniform. One big khaki family.

"I shouldn't have come."

"Don't be silly." He swivels. "You're family here. You know that."

He folds his hands together and makes his eyes sincere. It's a power some people have, they sort of wet their eyeballs and fill them with questioning. "Now tell me, what's been on your mind?"

"I want to know if this ever goes away. Do I have to become my mother?"

He laughs. "What else?"

"Is there any hope? Like those genius kids born in trailer courts — or at least some kind of free-will clause or something?"

"Though you refuse to form a complete sentence I think I understand your question, Eva."

He strokes his beard, the button-down, the stench of money. His clothes are ridiculous, really. Heisted right off an L.L. Bean mannequin. Nevertheless, they abuse her.

"Of course we have free will, and you are *not* your mother. But it seems you have inherited from her some ... *difficulties*, and they must be taken into account."

"I'm fucked."

"Stop that."

Eva shakes her head at the blue-diamond carpet.

"Look at me, will you?"

She won't.

"Now, listen — "

" — you know what I live with."

"I can't spend the rest of our lives insisting that it wasn't your fault, Eva. If you want to have any kind of life you are going to have to find a way to move past this."

"I haven't been taking my meds," she sniffs. "They keep me awake all night. My brain gets wrapped in a wet towel."

"Relax."

"I swear to God you could drive a nail into my hand and I wouldn't even flinch. I wouldn't."

Eva looks at her hands, guilty.

Fix it now.

"I stopped drinking coffee."

"That's good." He swivels. "And what else are you drinking?"

He means liquor.

"Eva, I don't have to tell you — "

"No. You don't."

"You know where that goes for you."

"Yes, I know. Thank you very much."

Collier leans back in his chair, sighs at the ceiling. Eva wonders how many times he is going to do that; lean back and sigh. She imagines him doing it many times in a row, over and over, breaking a sweat.

"What's so funny?"

She's laughing.

"I talk to you sometimes. In my head."

He straightens. "And who do you talk to in real life?"

"I haven't seen anyone. Not counting funerals — or bars. Guess I'm not really the first person you think to call when you want to have a good time."

He frowns. "I have something new for you to try. It's a young med at this point, so mum's the word."

"Fuck it," Eva says.

"Just try this one for me. It works well for a lot of people. I think it's worth a shot." Collier smiles and folds his hands. "We're gonna get it this time. I can feel it."

THE VISIT

The pharmacist gives Eva two mysterious bottles of pills. The bottles promise equanimity but once taken produce feelings of impending doom.

For the first two hours she does not lift her head from the pillow. Her skull is a granite paperweight. She lies in fever, swearing and hallucinating, bagpipes in the pillow. Each time she jumps from bed paranoid, pacing its edge and frisking the couch where the bagpipes are hidden, all sound is sucked out, leaving her with the terrible sensation of suffocating. The only way to breathe is to lie down and hear the bagpipes again. Eva Stark goes on like this for hours, jumping up and lying down. In the bathroom she opens bottles and begins swallowing. One of them will make her sleep.

EVA: I don't feel so hot.

COLLIER: You're having an allergic reaction.

EVA: I'm going to call 911.

COLLIER: Good. Don't get slippery, dear. You must punch only three numbers.

EVA: I really can't afford this.

COLLIER: I think it's important.

EVA: How can I tell if I'm dying?

COLLIER: Dry mouth, conversations with dead relatives, big bright light. That's what I hear, anyway.

When he first appears, he's all blue. Hung in the fig tree outside her living room window in a sort of cherub's repose, calm and stiff. He wears his burial clothes: the Ramones T-shirt, the white denim jacket. Almost four months have passed since they last met at the pine box. She presses her hand to the pane, and opens the window.

"I know you," she whispers, remembering the cedar beam and the long look he gave his feet.

Charles's mouth opens slowly as if to speak and she waits with great anticipation to recieve his message. Eva leans out, gripping the sill, offering her face to the aperture.

His eyes roll white, the deep of his mouth widening. It continues to open. His jaw unhooks from his head.

THE INTRODUCTION

This evening, they move together down her street, Charles a few feet ahead, driven. Eva likes his determination. The motion is effortless. Empty Sixth Avenue, the windows dark and noiseless. Past Fifth and Fourth toward the quiet pilgrimage of the Willamette.

The shadows, slain beside their buildings, pulse red under their black. Charles takes the sidestreet that dives below the bridge, the route of an appled worm. Above, a neon billboard flashes strange codes, troublesome numerologies. There is something to tell him, but the street is quickly becoming a dark bowl and swallows him. In an instant, he's irretrievable.

Eva enters the dark after him. Under the bridge, she begins to float. A sea of warm saline rushes to meet her. And then a touch of light swims to her pupil. And then another small scrap of light, and another. Slowly, the landscape undresses. Broken bottles sprout in the dirt, railroad ties rot in piles. And a figure, some fifty feet beyond, sways into focus. She squints, dizzy and overheated. The man floats toward her. The pill's symphony swells in her veins and he's suddenly on her. Her eyes darken, her knees begin to give. The body, autumnal, struggles to draw its cells to its center.

"Hello," she calls from deep water, extending her hand to him in the dark.

"Hello," says Caspar, taking it.

acknowledgements

Thanks to Dorien, Angel, Jason Glaser, Jorge, Charlie Salas Humara, Joe Kelly, Adrienne, Celeste, Peter Bauer, Eli Hopkins, and Portland for helping to inspire these essays. To my family: Paul Wells, Kim Anderson, and Prudence Johnston. To my other family: Timothy Kelly, Yael, Maria, Allison, Melanie Brown, Charlotte, and Jenny B. The title of this book comes from Ben's future brat punk band. Thanks to Ecotone, where The Body Autumnal first appeared in a different form (Volume 3, Number 2: Spring 2008). That story is dedicated to the memory of Matt Fitzgerald. Thanks to Sumanth, and Madras Press. Thanks to Justin Hocking, Michael D'Allesandro, A.M. O'Malley, and the IPRC. To Robert Braille, Walter Butts, Lydia Mazer, and Sarah Cypher for friendship and editorial advice. Thanks to Perfect Day for commissioning this work. Most of these essays were written at Hypatia in the Woods in October, 2010. Thanks to Elspeth Pope and the board of Hypatia for time, space, and a lovely house. Love and gratitude to my supports and fellow writers: Brit Washburne, Robbie Overbey, Julia Ain Krupa, Martha Grover, Jim Kinley, Aisha Edwards, Kristie L., Christine Palm, Hana Andronikova, and the Miller brothers.

Fall 2011 on Perfect Day Publishing

the collected
SOMNAMBULIST

Martha Grover ━━━━━━━

" ... *probably about the most awesome zine in the entire universe* ... "

Aaron Dietz, author of *Super*

"The dialogue is so honest and true ... we come to know this family better than we could have if it were told any other way ... the funniest thing I've read in a while."

Aron Nels Steinke, author of *Neptune*

WWW.SOMNAMBULISTZINE.BLOGSPOT.COM

Yeah. No. Totally. is set in Goudy Old Style, created by Frederic W. Goudy in 1915. With round curves and thin strokes, Goudy Old Style brings a gentle humanity to a document that might look too austere in a more workaday face.

Lisa Wells lives in Portland, Oregon.